Resurrected Heart

Leah N. Evans

Resurrected Heart

A Survival Journey

Based on a true story

LEAH N EVANS

ISBN:9798490767442

DEDICATION

This story is dedicated to the fallen victims of abuse and written to strengthen and enlighten those that dare to conquer unhealthy abusive relationships. As a survivor, I assure you that you have already won, you are loved, and you deserve nothing less than the love that only Christ can give. This non-fictional creative novel is told in 3rd person, and unlike a fictional novel, the story is based on actual events I experienced in the most devastating season of my life. If you have ever been a victim of abuse, please receive this prophetic word now; You have found real hope. I pray that as we embark on this journey together, you will gain strategies to stand in victory for a battle that the Lord has already won. Assume your inherited posture right now! You are living under the protective hand of Almighty God, and He is about to resurrect your broken heart.

TABLE OF CONTENTS

FORWARD
....

INTRODUCTION
....

CHAPTER 1   Cold Memories
....

CHAPTER 2   Family Ties
....

CHAPTER 3   Back-Home Holiday
....

CHAPTER 4   AAA: Alure, Anxiety,
Anguish ....

CHAPTER 5   Eye of the Storm
....

CHAPTER 6   Behold a New Thing
....

CHAPTER 7   Uprooted & Grounded
....

CHAPTER 8   Periwinkle Rag
....

CHAPTER 9   Down the Lane
....

CHAPTER 10 Holy Sake
....

CHAPTER 11 Whispering Revelation
....

CHAPTER 12 The Upper Room
Tarry ....

CHAPTER 13 Tender Heart
....

CHAPTER 14 Deceived Heart
....

CHAPTER 15 Terrorized Heart
....

CHAPTER 16   Reconciled to Bondage
....

CHAPTER 17   Accidental Backslide
....

CHAPTER 18 Deaths Defeat
....

CHAPTER 19   Called From the Grave
....

AFTERWORD
....

FOREWORD

My adoration and reverence for the invaluable Word of God will be expressed in its entirety through this story told in 3rd person. I trust that you as the reader will be blessed with a seamless and fluent revelation, much like the divine revelation I experienced in writing what God placed on my heart. It is highly recommended that you meditate on the scriptures proceeding each chapter while reading this powerful story. I take no credit for this piece of literature. It is very humbling that God chose to use me, despite all my imperfections, to deliver what I know is destined to be a blessing for those that receive it.

This story is just a snippet of my life's journey. These were critical events that compounded my sufferings, joys, hardships, faith, and spiritual growth. It is the harrowing chronicle of my walk out of "true adultery" and down the aisle to Christ.

I am thankful for the opportunity to share some

of my life's most intimate moments in a non-fictional narrative that is closely based on my journey through an abusive marriage. I pray that each reader can view my personal story as one to relate to, empathize with, and glean from. My journey is a direct reflection of my personal walk with my maker, husband, redeemer, and savior, Jesus Christ. As much as this book is my personal story through my surrender, it is God's story of His redemptive work in my life to honor and glorify Him. My prayer is that the divine revelations included in this narrative serve to help you find your own personal intimacy with our loving God, and my story of hardship and suffering can serve as a revelation to each one of you. I pray that it will help you to walk in the fruits of the spirit: greater love, joy, peace, long-suffering, goodness, faithfulness, kindness, gentleness, and self-control.

Each of you has his or her own divine purpose and path regardless of how the Lord has led me. I can only pray that my testimony serves as the same flickering candlelight that gently lit the isle for me, as I walked to wed my Lord and my groom. May you experience that same essence of light as we journey together. Whether you are on a dark road, you have lost your way on a dead-end road, or you cannot see the deadly snares on the foggy path ahead: Wherever you are and whomever you are, may this collection of words divinely light your path in a supernatural way.

The Spirit led inspiration of this writing came from a revelation given to me by Christ during our engagement. It may not be one that everyone can readily accept or understand because it is graphic! However, because my faith knows that it is God-breathed, it must be told. This is the journey through a battle that was conquered long before it began. Afterward, I would like to share a heartbreaking testimony with you about other women I know that did not survive the abuse. I am fully confident that by sharing these horrifying events, my story will have a much greater impact. For those of you facing the yokes of abusive bondage, it is only the anointing of God's living Word that can break the yoke. Hold on tight as we enter the harrowing story of Lilly and Oliver.

Introduction

"One thing I ask from the Lord, this only do I seek: that I may dwell in the house of the Lord all the days of my life, to gaze on the beauty of the Lord and to seek Him in His temple."

– Psalms 27:4- (BSB)

Outside of the seven long painful years of marriage; outside of suppressing many years of denial; outside of forcing justification for the sake of reverencing a few dear, yet happy memories; outside of the intense withdrawals of loneliness, this is where she stood. Far gone from overwhelming depression that made her question how she could continue to face the world; far gone from hoping inside of an impossible love, she stood enraptured by the very presence of God. Lovesick, in awe, and overcome by an immense gratefulness for every breath, she was continually extended moment after moment, the ability to repeat that same grace. Basking in the spirit that was breathing on her, He welcomed her with a warm embrace, and she received Him with thanksgiving. He infiltrated her heart and penetrated her spirit until she fluttered with weakness. One could say she acquiesced to an intrusive submission that made all she ever was and all that she ever would be, yield to His power: A power more than worthy of serving; a power almighty and irrevocable; a power majestically strong; a power that encapsulates all these characteristics, yet concurrently remained gentle. She would always know Him. Even though she had experienced a brush of His euphoria in her youth, it had been forgotten; tucked away as if for necessity; tucked away that she might invoke to lean upon it, outside of the upside of worldliness. It would not just be remembered going forward, but it would be ever present: veiling and sheltering her with antecedence.

Between falling outside of herself and falling out of love with all but His power, this glorious presence managed to eclipse the memory of pain and humiliation, anger and unworthy feelings, every distrust, and all the things that made her die to abundant life. A feathering sensation that came from an inhaled breath, not exhaled at once, but withheld and overcome by His penetrating Spirit gently stroking her at the sides of her breast. It traced the shape of her hips until her feet were weak and unsteady; until they trembled with uncertainty; until she felt as if they could no longer hold her upright. Yet, the Spirit which paralyzed her flesh was indeed able to thrust her into the heights of Heaven.

An old, yet familiar Spirit that came with a fresh newness to weaken her. To pounce upon and revive her straightaway. Bowing her head and shoulders in submission, she finally decided to fully die to all that she was. The saturating spirit would blow with force, until she cried out to rebirth all that would become. Right there, surrendering her life again; she surrendered all of her past, present and future as well. Her heart had been resurrected. She would love like never before, and like never again and forever more. Inside of His mighty arms, her heart was resurrected to new life. Her heart would live and die for Him, as though it was buried alive. All of this she would soon find out, but a death had to occur before there could be a resurrection.

CHAPTER I

Cold Memories

"Brothers, I do not consider myself yet to have taken hold of it. But one thing I do: Forgetting what is behind and straining toward what is ahead."

- Philippians 3:13- (BSB)

He had been gone for close to 6 months. The routines of living and family traditions they had conceived together were coy in reminiscence. For once, the Holiday season came with the promise of an unfamiliar peace. It was an invigorating feeling to have no anticipation of the intense strife she had come to know. It perpetually stifled the aura of warmth, sharing, and giving that personified the spirit of the season. The loneliness she felt was drowned out by the familiar harmony of what a joyous season felt like in her youth. As she walked through the mall, she admired the lighting that glowed through the large ceiling windows. They shined bright upon the small young family sitting for lunch in the food court. Beaming warm rays of brilliant sunlight contradicted the chill of the season outside. The scent of cinnamon, cloves, pine, and citrusy spices surreptitiously emerged as she strolled past the bustling crowds at the entrance of Macy's. From the east wing of the mall, she was headed westward toward one of her favorite inner isle booths. There were so many people present; some rushing to make quick purchases on a lunchbreak; some casually strolling to explore and select intentional or impromptu items. It was the usual bustling Holiday crowd. Lilly never came to the mall to do any intensive shopping. She would often meet Oliver at the food court for lunch since this was the median location between their places of employment. They were always cordial for these brief sit-downs, quickly confirming dinner plans for later or venting about the flow of their hectic days. They would make jokes about the passers-by, while filling each other in on incoming phone calls from distant relatives, bill collectors, or solicitors. Sometimes, on non-workdays, they would come just to grab a pair of ear studs for Oliver, or a new pair of shades for her collection. He would always buy her the jazziest shades, usually out of guilt for the most recent black eye or facial bruise he had inflicted. She shook the memories as she approached her destination.

The booth employee who happened to be a member of her church greeted her.

"Hey Lilly, where is Brother O?"

She again shrugged past the frightful memories and replied,

"Oh, he's somewhere in his skin."

She knew Bobby would counter her response with further investigation as she had abandoned regular church attendance since 'O' had left 6 months ago. Quickly anticipating the oncoming interrogation, Lilly launched her own line of questioning.

"So how is Beatrice and the boys? Let her know that I'm almost done

with that book she loaned me, and I'll get it back to her soon."

This was enough to make him shift his query to a personal family update.

"Will do. Oh, they are growing. Percy just had a birthday last week, and

Pauls got his license and a girlfriend now."

With the successful shift in conversation, she began to browse the booth for her favorite scented oils. They were alphabetized and easy to locate. Bobby finished his declaration, and then interjected to assist.

"What can I help you find today Lil?"

Sniffing a fragrant new scent, she answered,

"Do you have any more Egyptian Musk? I think I grabbed the last Jersey
by Chanel."

He took the keys draped around his neck and opened the locked cabinet under the booth's cash register. After fumbling through the storage compartments, Bobby pulled out a Ziploc bag filled with small bottles of the requested scent and handed her one. She opened it to sniff and approve. They swopped cash and paper bag simultaneously just as another customer interjected with perfect timing.

"What do you recommend for older gentlemen?"

Lily smiled in relief, waved, and walked off silently, dipping into the meandering current of shoppers. She headed back toward the entrance where she had parked and stopped to purchase a cup of hot chocolate to combat the chilly wind that awaited her upon exiting. She pulled down her hat, grabbed the change, and gripping the warm cup of steaming chocolate, headed for home. As Lilly walked carefully to avoid spilling her drink, just ahead, the high spewing fountain of the Mall's wishing pool came into view. Thinking about how many times she had purchased "better" with the toss of a coin, she secretly calculated at least $5.00 on a better marriage, at least $3.00 on a more loving relationship, and $3.00 for more sensitivity. Oh, and how could she forget the $2 bucks additionally for happiness, and at least $1.75 to retract every stupid wish for "better" in exchange for a chance to start all over again. Lilly realized that she had wasted time wishing that 'better' would majestically pop out of that fountain as easily as the coins were flipped in: Wishing that the hope of "better" she chucked in, would be raptured into a large rush of water surging in an upward cascade, and find its way into reality like the few tiny drops that landed on the pool's concrete ledge. Small chance, but not impossible. She thought it all naïve now. The false advertising of other wish buyers with closed eyes, and glistening promises would not sway her to believe that another wish was worth half a cent. As she pushed open the door to exit the building, Lilly took what would have normally been her wish allowance and tossed it slightly in her hand. She felt better depositing it into the large red collection kettle swinging in the frosty air. The missionary elf ringing his bell outside of the Mall's main entrance smiled with gratitude. "Happy Holidays," she responded as her mental effort refocused to muster up a slight grin. The outdoor chill froze every recent thought of the past, and she quickly rushed to her car to escape its overbearing bitterness.

CHAPTER II

Family Ties

"But as for you, be strong; do not be discouraged,
for your work will be rewarded."

– 2 Chron 15:7- (BSB)

It had been the first time in over 10 years that
Lilly spent the Holidays with her family. When she
decided to leave New York to come to Georgia, her
intention was to just venture off and experience
something different. There were so many benefits
to living in the south. It was cheaper, the weather
was much milder, and the pace of life was never
rushed. People in the south took a little more time
to do things. She recalled this slower pace being
an annoyance at first. Waiting at the DMV in a
fast-paced city was excruciating enough with the
automated number systems that announced the
next patron's turn on the large, mounted monitors.
It made the process speedier and more efficient,
but you could still expect to spend 2 hours for

any minor transaction. Unfortunately, the small county offices in the south lacked the technology of the northern cities. A woman would typically hand patrons a small yellow post-it with a handwritten number on it when they walked in. After a seated wait that made your butt cheeks numb, another woman would call out your post-it number to proceed to a designated service line. The antiquated process was much slower without modern technology but adjusting to the slow pace came with time.

Lilly was a good cook. She prepared many Holiday meals alone as an adult, recalling the traditional recipes her grandmother and mother had mastered after years of watching the preparation. The ladies would always help with the prep work, chopping bell peppers, onions, and garlic. She recalled being the little girl selected to assist Great Granny Darling in collecting fresh herbs from a small herb garden in front of the house. It gave her a sense of pride and made her feel smart because you had to know how to read to help with this special task. None of the other cousins had been promoted to this position yet. They were only allowed to hold the collection basket to carry what she was told to find and pick. So, the others would anxiously await with envious hearts. In a while, the 'Big Easter Egg Hunt' would afford them the opportunity to show off their seek and find skills so that they could eventually be recruited as real garden assistants. They convinced themselves that the Easter roundup was better anyway because some of the eggs were plastic and filled with chocolate and chewy sweet finds that they loved to eat.

"Who wants to pick yucky herbs?"

Lilly chuckled as she remembered the gripes of her sister who always coveted the important garden maid job.

Now that they were grown, they could mix blackberry brandy and orange juice while they whipped, mixed, and chopped. They could get caught up on each other's lives and tell funny stories about their Holidays apart. All in the company of their mother, who they would use constantly as a reference to get things right amid their social distractions. Mom would make sure they set proper oven temperatures and times, and she would give correct ingredient measurements as she delighted in seeing her now grown daughters together again. The male cousins and sons would be on standby with alert noses, rubbing their hands together, and licking their lips with anticipation of taste testing everything: Especially the family traditional favorites like the old-fashioned sage dressing and rich sweet potato pie filling.

The young adults would remember old times and create new memories together after many years apart. Reminiscing over the fondest and most comical memories of their elders who had passed away, they'd recall their youthful woes caused by disobedience and teenage mischief. Mother enjoyed watching the family collectively share their joys, hopes, and sorrows, and revel in all that they had missed in each other's lives. It was like being back home again; like Deja vu.

She settled in her basking and decided to get up early to start the day. It was about 7 am. Everyone was still asleep after their 16-hour van ride from up north. Lilly threw on her robe and quietly tip-toed out of her room, down the hall, and into the kitchen. The alternating rhythm of snoring that came from both sofas in the living room dimmed the guilt she felt for noisily fumbling around in the kitchen, running water to make fresh coffee, and clanging pots to retrieve a pan for cooking break-fast. Having the whole family visit for the Holidays was such a joy. She decided to compassionately delay her intentions to maintain the reticent morn-ing setting. It would be best to quietly prepare a cup of coffee and step onto the back porch.

It was a cool morning, but not cold. She could immediately tell that later in the day, the tempera-ture would reach the upper 50's, or lower 60's. It was easy to get acquainted with the weather in the south, and just as easy to forget the bitter cold windy days of winters back home. Lilly took a deep breath as she stood and admired the sight of the rippling lake beyond the tall pine trees just a few yards away. It was too late for sunrise, but all the same, the aura of a brand-new day was refreshing.

Later, she would bring the children out in search for pinecones to spray paint and decorate into little Christmas trees. The boys could rake and gather the pine straw to garnish the beds of hedges surrounding the front porch. If there was time, maybe she could go into the storage room and pull out the Holiday wreaths for the windows and doors.

She ventured off eastward, quietly walking through the unfenced yard of her neighbor. The adjacent house would soon be her mother's new home. Still empty, it was a small quaint cookie-cutter ranch with a layout identical to her own home. She thought about what kind of surprise could be placed inside to make her mother smile; something that the entire family could make good use of. Nothing came to mind immediately, but she knew that this would be her project for the day. Lilly peeked into the back door and glimpsed at the living room and kitchen area. It needed curtains and window treatments, but that would be an aside. After heading back to the house and showering, she took a seat out on the back patio and set a fresh cup of coffee down while continuing to brainstorm about her mother's housewarming surprise. The rippling water of the lake, the steam from the coffee, and the excitement of the family gathering brought a warm smile to Lilly's heart. in that moment, the importance of her family never mattered more.

CHAPTER III

Back-Home Holiday

Jesus looked at them and said, "With man this is impossible, but with God all things are possible."

- Matthew 19:26- (BSB)

It was move in day for her mom and other family members. Lilly managed to furnish the home enough to make it comfortable to live in. It was shaping up to be a very Merry Christmas, just like the days of old.

She was absolutely thrilled with the Gingerbread house that the children crafted while drinking hot chocolate and sharing ideas. So adorable, with its peanut brittle walkway and chocolate coated rice crispy treat fire logs. The logs were stacked up against the pretzel stick and Tootsie Roll jointed fence in its back yard. The Gingerbread house was meticulously detailed with halved vanilla Tootsie Roll shingles to resemble a snow-covered roof, and white cotton candy around the base for a snowy yard. She poked at the children's imaginations leading them in creating this glorious peppermint wreathed, gumdrop light-posted wonderland. It was the perfect center piece for the grand oak dining room table set Lilly had purchased for her mother's housewarming holiday surprise. The upside-down Santa feet sticking out of the top of the gingerbread chimney made her giggle at heart. While that was jolly, a more heartrending glee came to her while admiring the tiny candy yard nativity scene that sat in the front corner next to a decorated candy tree. It pained her to think of throwing it away after the Holiday season passed. She had already photographed every angle of the masterpiece so they would always have the memory of every minute detail. Still, she grabbed her phone to do one last fair-well finale photoshoot for pride's sake.

Lilly had prepared dinner at her house, and secretly had the guys transport the finished dishes one house over to her mother's vacant bungalow. They would surprise mom with a meal graced upon this second hand but lovely old country table, with retractable leaves that could seat eight. Her mother was ecstatic, surprised, and pleased when she laid eyes on the beautifully set table. It was just her mother's style, and her vision for all future accommodating décor would flow from its down-home antique fashion.

Everyone was busy transporting their belongings

from Lilly's house to her mother's ranch. There was nothing too heavy, and they didn't bring in much for now. The van was still fully loaded from top to inside with large suitcases, and carefully stacked boxes and totes. A small hauling trailer full of more light items was hitched to the back. As she finished admiring the Gingerbread house, Lilly pocketed her phone and grabbed a heavy laundry basket from her tiny niece who struggled to see her way in the front door. She placed it on the used washer that was just purchased along with the dining room set. It was best to gift the washer to her mom as well after realizing her laundry room was too small, and it was still filled with Oliver's belongings. She had found the table and washer on sale at the second-hand thrift shop midtown. The dining room table set probably came from the home of an older couple's estate sale. Although old, it was in great condition. The washer looked a bit more worn, but it was sturdy and would be great for heavy duty washing to accommodate both houses. Lilly felt blessed that she had spent less than $300 for both items: Some small miscellaneous perks like storage baskets and Tupperware containers were thrown in complimentary. It was obvious that these small starter items gave her family a sense of settlement, and new beginnings.

She walked back to her house and stood at her back-bedroom window, where underneath it, the Bible layed open on top of a nightstand. The last scripture read was in the book of Psalms during her daily evening prayer. Lilly looked out at the lake and realized that it was different: Much different! On the news a few days earlier, she recalled seeing a broadcast about the work that had been done to repair a water dam. This construction had obviously affected the lakes water level drastically. Amid the lake where it always looked like the waters were abyssal in depth, sections of muddy earth could be seen in between puddles of water. It looked as if you could skip earthy section by earthy section right into the middle of the subsided water, and if you dared, right through to the opposite shore to the east. The receded lake exposed the mud bed that stretched back up a path where the water was waned clear to the opposite bank. It appeared as though a lake had never existed there at all.

Falling into a state of immediate awe, the epiphany of Moses parting the Red Sea became less majestic and more divinely pragmatic. She had always wondered just how miraculous it must have been when Joshua and the twelve men stood in the midst of the Jordan with the twelve stones. These Biblical scenes felt more realistic as she watched the vicariousness of the receded lake. She wondered about her own personal Promised Land. What did it look like? Would she ever stand on its banks? She peered out over the scene and viewed a grand, slate gray four story home which sat on the opposite bank. It appeared stately with its imperial white windowpanes, the only structure of its kind in view. Its foundation sat hidden beyond the thick foliage that created a forested border. The shrubbery peaked low from the left and towered to the right. The grounds of the home appeared mysteriously elegant, and the landscape sophisticatedly modern in its architectural design. Would her Canaan be as glorious? Would she ever arrive? The muddy patches of land once totally immersed made the possibility of one day arriving just that: Possible! Lilly had survived a brutal trek through the wilderness, and the promise of a new land filled her soul with hope. She lastingly inhaled the damp morning mist of precipitating dew. It became one with her internal river of living water. Her exhaled spirit believed in a brighter future, and a newly watered faith made it so. But the past still haunted her visions of a promised land filled with milk and honey.

CHAPTER IV

AAA: Allure, Anxiety, Anguish

"Wine is a mocker, strong drink is a brawler, and
whoever is led astray by them is not wise."
- Proverbs 20:1- (BSB)

No peace was within. In fact, she was overcome
with just the opposite: Anxiety! Oliver had been
gone for three days and each day brought a more
vivid reality. Her agitation tortured every waking
thought. As much as Lilly attempted to redirect her
focus, she could not escape drowning in discord.
Unsatisfied with the visions of being alone, and
regretfully pondering all the attempts she could
have made to avoid this fate, she grew sick. There
was an actual conflict physically moving inside and
overwhelming her with uneasiness: Inescapable
stomach churns with disagreeing bile for her lack
of ability to avoid all that led to this. Lilly literally
became nauseous. A tangible anguish of chemis-
try inside needed to be purged. With a water-

ing mouth, she knew that this wasn't just mental disgust. The anguish manifested from her subconscious mind, and she gagged at its introduction. No longer able to contain the torture, she fled down the hall just in time to discharge what seemed like an unlimited pungent distress. Once Lilly had physically depleted all that she could, there remained the psychological essence of turmoil so intense, it haunted her soul.

Her mind was clouded with a commotion of contending actions which could have countered the tempest of her overwhelming regrets: Withstanding one more random inebriated insult: Negating the indignity by attributing it to the obvious addictions and mental instability. His rigid unpredictable criticisms where familiar enough to be taken as routine. It wasn't like this behavior was new or unusual. It was as if she had mastered the art of dismissing the attacks. After years of ignoring her existence, her relevance, her right to be respected, and her worthiness to be esteemed, Lilly had lost every ounce of her vivaciousness. What once appeared as if it could be shifted, gradually became a hopeless, dead-end chasm. The momentum of hopeful energy dwindled down to apathy; a detachment that made her surrender to every jab and joust.

Her recollection of submissive surrender made it more painful to admit that she had allowed circumstances to escalate to this level. Haunted by the reality that her anticipation of relief for his absence was fictitious, she was torn apart that whether she stood up for herself or submitted to his motives, she could not gain a sense of adoration; not from him, and not for herself either. Lilly was simply lost in the fluctuation of loneliness, disappointment, desperation, hurt, love, anger, tolerance, and remorse. The ebb and flow of emotions in her marriage had become a whirlwind of unsettling storms: Just as unpredictable as Oliver's anger, moods, or physical attacks.

The anxiety of it all kept her pacing as she did different household tasks, not focused enough to complete any one of them. She started in the laundry room and recalled an argument they recently had about missing an anniversary dinner that a friend invited them to. She escaped the thought and abandoned the load of clothes that needed to be dried. Lilly went into the kitchen and turned on the water. As it ran over her hands, she took her wet palm and wiped her face attempting to stop the tears before they started. She tested the heat of the water in preparation of washing the dishes. Upon commencing, she cleaned only a few plates, and washed a glass placing it on the dishrack to dry next to his burly beer mug. It made her want a drink knowing what most likely awaited in the hours ahead.

Lilly had unconsciously abandoned another chore. Pouring some chilled wine in the freshly washed glass, she sat at her dining room table, hoping that the drink would give her instant relief. She usually drank heavily on the nights that they would be intimate to numb her hurt and bitterness. The liquor would always help in heightening her allure and seductiveness. She had become a master at concocting spells with various love potions. They sometimes contained brandy and flavored coke, cognac and orange juice, or vodka and cranberry juice; always heavy on the alcohol just to make the love trans intoxicating and lasting. Lilly kept in mind that an unbalanced recipe could lead to disaster. If formulated exactly right, she would feel no anger or resentment, and the same spell would be cast on Oliver. The perfect love potion always produced passionate love making which would be obliterated from both of their memories when day broke. The intoxicated morning hangover ensured they wouldn't be able to resume a passion quickly forgotten. Even with fulfilling penetration just before sunrise, their souls would only get close enough to harmoniously interact with each other for a few days after at best. By the weekend, the love spell would be broken and had to be cast all over again. Bruised and aggrieved, she would be forced to get numb again and bewitched into becoming magically provocative and irresistibly enticing: All for a new round of a painfully inebriated fantasy. Unable to focus, Lilly decided to create a sleeping potion. She poured another glass of wine and opened the cabinet above the refrigerator to retrieve some brandy. After setting the bottle on the table and grabbing a seat, she tried to intoxicate herself enough to doze off. Her mind wandered to the last satisfying memory of 'O'. It was the last time they had touched, and she managed to hold fast to it: Mainly because it was one of the rare encounters that didn't fall into a painful abyss. Glimpses of this interaction were repeatedly jogged in her memory as she wrestled insanely with her new loneliness. Now fully intoxicated, Lilly could focus on nothing else as she went back to that night fully in her dizzied mind.

Gazing off into a corner, she slowly drifted back into the past: She had showered and groomed herself thoroughly, anticipating him arriving late that night. Oliver had to work a double and she knew he would be exhausted. It was highly possible that he would be irritated as well. Good strategy would require creating the perfect centerpiece on the square glass kitchen tabletop. A bottle of smooth rum, an ice bucket, candles, and deep indigo glasses would set the right mood. It would be an absolute necessity: The sign of relief he would surely need upon entering the back door and heading into the kitchen. Some soft R & B music would help, so she popped five of his favorite mellow CDs into the stereo. Lilly scented the house with lavender and vanilla to balance out the intense aromas of smothered pork chops with onions and garlicy green beans. No scent, however, would compete with the Obsession oil that she had rubbed into her skin. It mimicked a butterscotch infused bergamot, with a bold vanilla and amber undertone. Intoxicating to say the least, it was sexy and irresistibly sweet. She slipped on a satin royal blue gown which was laced across the breast line and thigh hem, with teal laced panties and bra boldly hidden underneath. Lilly slid some beautiful heals on over red painted toes, then added dangling diamond earrings as a final touch. The perfect tactics to mesmerize and mellow him before sending a sexually laden text message. That would set the tone for the evening.

She recalled the events as though they had occurred yesterday.

"Hey 'O', you said you would be home by 11:00. Should I draw you a

hot bath, or would you like to eat first?"

No immediate response. That was not a good sign.

It was 10:45 and in the pit of her belly, there arose a desperate hope that the house would not soon become the scene of another crime. She finished up her makeup, deciding on a deep rouge sparkling gloss that needed no touching up once disturbed. Going with a subtle natural look was the evening choice. Neutral yet bold in the eyes. After doing a once over, she left the bathroom checking the mirror first, and then the overall scene to ensure the candles were in place and ready to be lit. Lilly recalled entering the bedroom and turning back the comforter of the neatly made bed to reveal the satin red sheets. They matched the abundance of stacked pillows, all giving an invitation to a sexually charged evening of comfort and ecstasy. Candles were in place there on the bedside as well. She left the door to the half bath slightly jarred to give off a gentle spotlight effect on the bed. His black silk pajama pants, boxer briefs, and an optional sleeveless white tee laid neatly across the bed's lower corner.

Oliver finally responded.

"I need a drink. What's there at the house? Do I need to make a stop?"

She wasn't surprised, but immediately snapped into a state of awareness, knowing that her plan could easily fall apart if not played just right. Lilly walked into the kitchen and nervously poured a little brandy for herself. Glass in one hand and phone in the other, she quickly responded back.

"Everything you need is already here. Just waiting on you."

Familiar with his ways, she presumed that he had been proactive enough to head to the liquor store anyway. In her mind, there was another desperate hope that he didn't come home with the cheap vodka he always opted for. That was usually O's booze of choice because it was plentiful for little to nothing. It never went down easy, and it always seemed to regurgitate into projectile rage and hatred: But Lilly knew what she was facing, so playing it smart was crucial.

She went and sat in the corner of the scarcely occupied den, the last place he would look for her. It was a room that they used mostly to entertain guests. Her subconscious thoughts wanted to hide from the anticipation of what her intuition foresaw: Complaints that invoked defensive remarks, which always provoked his bitter and harsh comments. All of this would usually metamorphosize into verbal combat, eventually leaving her defeated and in physical pain. "Not tonight," Lilly recalled thinking to herself. The plan was about to be activated.

She recalled quickly walking through the house and lighting all the candles. There was a gulp of another round of strong liquor, and a retreat to her concealed corner with a helping of a powerful love potion concocted just for Oliver. He finally pulled up in the driveway. She heard him slam the car door and head past the den window next to her seat in the back entrance of the house. With a racing heart and a deep fearful breath, she heard him unlock the door. Lilly bounced her right leg over her left leg nervously swinging it to and fro. She would wait for him to scope out the scene of the night she had prepared. Then he would hopefully come to find her being pleased with the romantic setup. It was usually hit or miss, but one thing was certain. These initial moments always caused inner turmoil, and a stirring of extreme anxiety.

Already enchanted with her own intoxication, there was no doubt the spell that was about to be cast would succeed. She heard him place a bottle on the counter before walking down the hall. Lilly waited intensely; prepared for passion; full of loving care; ready to overwhelm and capture him. It took a lengthy moment for Oliver to come back to the kitchen area. Waiting for him to come into her presence, he decided to detour back to the counter where he had left his goods. 'O' called for her, and in perfect timing, she arose and showed herself. She stepped into the middle of the room with her sexy appearance on full display. As he turned around, Lilly recalled stepping forward. When Oliver spotted her, he froze and smiled from ear to ear. She gracefully and seductively glided into the room before him and immediately spotted the drink that he had poured for himself. Wisdom would be required if her plan were to work. Lilly smoothly took the cheap vodka from him and sipped it as she handed 'O' the pre-mixed love potion. She swallowed the strong spirits with a lip perking shivery response, and then placed the glass on the table hoping it would be forgotten. He turned up the potion he was given and quickly consumed it as he looked at her with anticipation. So far so good, but after setting the empty glass down, Oliver reached for the one she had conned from him. He turned it up as she began to undress him, belt first. After placing the emptied glass down, he said, "I've been waiting for you all day." She replied, "I can see," as he responded with a smirk. Lilly knew she would win the enchanted battle tonight. The spell altered sexual fight would be exactly what she had conjured up: Nothing like the physical fights that usually ensued. She tilted her head, took a deep breath, and gazed into his eyes as she unbuttoned his pants. He was solid already, weapon drawn and ready for combat.

She whispered, with a conniving gesture,

"How should we begin?"

Oliver placed one hand at the back of her neck as he completely stripped out of his pants, aiding the execution of her first war tactic. Gently rubbing his chest, she leaned in to kiss him, continuing her careful inquiry.

"Like this?" Just as he responded with

"Yes, just like…",

her lips pulled on his bottom lip and then the top.

She had struck the first timid blow: Soft but daring. They slowly began to engage in a passionate brawl that would last all night. Lilly was ready for this sexual war, always aware that a wrong move could turn it into a nightmare. It would be another marathon endurance game filled with various battles, various positions of combat, and various battlefields. Still holding her neck, Oliver moved one of her hands slowly down his torso. This gave her full access to his weapon, placing it right in her grasp. "Easy win," she thought. He viciously bit and pinched at her neck with his mouth. Drawing in her irresistible scent, he became more eager to engage her. The counterattack was swift as Lilly began to bite down on his breast plate. The wet warmth of her aggression insinuated that blood had been drawn, and the pain was glorious. He threw his head back in agony. Eager to contend, Oliver pressed the back of her neck, driving Lilly down his torso, to her knees in surrender. He pried her mouth open with an extraordinarily powerful neck grip. 'O' began stabbing her throat forcefully. His sword rested firmly on her wet flesh as it painfully carved into her orifice. Knowing she would regain the momentum after he physically expelled some of his energy, Lilly endured the pain of successive tear-jerking stabs. She withstood the misery of ever bloody wet blow. Welcoming his fierce penetration knowing that she wouldn't be defeated, she gasped for air. It was time to strategically act as if she had lost this round. Once Oliver immerged confidently victorious in his exhaustive assault, she seized the opportunity to regain her stance. Injured but still able, Lilly rested her face on his thighs: One more act of trickery as she calculated her next fierce blow. She rose to her feet appearing deceptively wounded, as her body collapsed into his: A cunning acknowledgment that she accepted defeat, while mentally preparing for the continuation of this exhausting battle. The calculated move was to withdraw and retreat.

Imitating a truce, she lured her opponent into the dim candlelit bathroom. This would be the next battleground to recommence the duel. She took the hand of her exhausted opponent and sat him on the curb of the tub. Lilly leaned over to run the water, and 'O' ran his hand down the small of her back. He grabbed at her hips until she was straddled over him. He wanted her to win the next round. Exhausted from sprawling, Oliver pressed his face into her belly and hung from her waist with both arms, appearing desperately drained and unable to resume. He would surrender before the fight. Once again, she was in the perfect position to inflict injury, but she knew it was not necessary to conquer him in his weakened state. Lilly was instinctively aware that even the slightest blow would resume the assault. That could risk distracting her from initiating the next part of the battle plan, which was critical for defeat. She gripped his head with both hands, showing that she was in control. Standing over him to show honor for a fight well fought, she slowly broke contact and backed away in retreat. There was little doubt that he would remain seated on the tub to regain strength.

Lilly put on her robe and quickly went to retrieve another spell bottle. This time, she mixed up a different love potion: One that would activate a playful giddy passion. She sipped a heavy dose of the potion and brought a glass into the bathroom for Oliver. He was already undressed and standing in the shower exhausted, yet relieved and refreshed. She pulled the curtain back to hand him the glass of passion punch that had already begun to take a reenchanting effect on her. He sipped and was instantly enthralled and energize by this sweet elixir. Oliver looked at her with a youthful deviousness, and a cunning smirk. He clearly desired to pursue her as if they were middle aged children on a playground. Lilly's girl like naivety made her curious about his mood and intentions. It was obvious that his adrenaline was rushing as he turned the glass up. After guzzling down the passion punch, he placed the glass on the shower windowsill. Oliver grabbed her by her hand and still robbed, he aggressively yanked her into the shower. She resisted with a squeamish annoyance at what he had done, but his fun-loving spirit quickly softened her. He tickled the sides of her hips, wrapping his arms around her underneath the heavily saturated robe. Lilly hopped up onto him, wrapping her legs around his waist. The bout began again as the new spell came alive in him. She allowed 'O' to take the lead knowing that they were in a different space.

This time, he would be the playful young lad eager for a fun-filled adventure that would exhaust them both beyond revival when all was said and done.

He dipped at the hips to hold her up steadily, and his hand-free probing delightfully excited her. Lilly slid out of the saturated garment by leaning back with her arms downs. Oliver caught her, positioning one hand between her shoulder blades, while tightening his grip around her waist. Just as the heavy garment fell, he spun her around, and her wet hair slapped the side of his face in surprise. She gripped him around his broad shoulders to gain stability. Oliver quickly rested one foot on the tub curb. He dipped at the hips once more, bouncing her higher to meet more comfortably in the middle as she came down. Pressing all his weight on the elevated foot, 'O' tightened his thigh muscles before lifting himself up into a strong stable stance. As their bodies met amid her gravity and his inertia, Lilly's face filled with shock as he unexpectedly jolted them together. As her mouth opened wide in awe, he sensed her pain. Oliver rushed to sooth her by softly brushing his cheek and nose against the side of her face. She was easily forgiving and recaptured into play, as he danced her around gently, swaying her back and forth, round and round. No longer concerned that he had caused any major injury, he suddenly heightened the intensity of their love battle. Lilly was relaxed in his arms, brushing her lips and cheeks back and forth upon his moist shoulder. Abruptly, with no warning to her, 'O' grabbed her tightly, sat on the tub curb, and started to sharply bounce her up and down onto his lap. Up again and down again, over and over, he was checking to see how she would respond to his roughhouse playing. There was much more intensity this time. The aggression shocked her at first, but Lilly soon fell into his fun as he spoke to her in perfect rhythm with the elevated bouncing. She felt like a little toddler being tossed into the air: Anxious to come down and go back up again for more of the tummy tingling feel she would get each time. Enduring the pain, she enjoyed every upward thrust. When his arms grew heavy, she took over, bouncing herself up and down, bracing upon his shoulders, and allowing him to rest a bit and enjoy their fun as well. Lilly was the perfect competitor in this love battle they were playing. She challenged his sayings with a loving wittiness that made him want to compete even more. Oliver was slowly overcome by her strength as she bit her bottom lip showing her determination for continuity. Her adrenaline assisted her galloping, and suddenly, his facial expression switched from awe to pain. Lilly was in command now, confident that he was strong enough to endure her bully bouncing. It was payback time, and she would injure him just enough to win the game before consoling him. His expression then switched from pain back to awe, then to relief once she finally settled into his lap. Her legs trembled with exhaustion. Lilly tucked her nose into the side of his neck and panted heavily, confident that she had worn him out completely. Suddenly, to her surprise, he jumped up with her in his arms to continue romping around! All she could do was laugh. He tossed her into a cradle position as he viciously nibbled at her neck. The combination of ticklishness, surprise, and exhaustion made Lilly burst into insatiable laughter, and finally a desperate squealing plea for his resignation. She recalled Oliver shouting,

"Trampoline time,"

as he suddenly broke from the slippery bathroom floor toward the bed.

Coming back out of her memory, she was saddened at the thought of rough, but good times like these that seemed so rare because most were lost in an inebriated abyss. Other encounters were overcome by episodes of agonizing dreadful terror, and unimaginable violence. Why couldn't these brutal battles be lost in the abyss too? Lilly wanted this so desperately, but she refused to allow her mind to go back into those dark memories of mental anguish, and painful bruises. Horrible moments that were vivid but had to be drowned out: Much like the drunken causes that led to these injuries and broken moments. It would be such a relief to just toss out all their memories; the good, bad, beautiful, and ugly, into a black dimension of the unknown. If they could only be stricken from any reality of hers; eliminated out of existence totally. A place where he, nor she, ever existed, ever met, or ever fell in love.

Lilly cried for the sparce joy of it all, and the never-ending pain of it all. She cried for the agony of knowing love with her enemy and shed tears for the joy of escaping an inevitable fate: Giving way to every emotion that came with the thoughts of who they once were together, and who they now were apart. Suddenly she realized that she didn't know what to feel, or how to cope. All she could think of was who could help.

"God help me," she cried.

"Lord please help me."

"So let us come boldly to the throne of our gracious God. There, we will receive his mercy, and we will find grace to help us when we need it most."

-Heb 4:16- (NLT)

CHAPTER V

Eye of the Storm

"Why are you downcast, O my soul? Why the
unease within me? Put your hope in God, for I
will yet praise Him, my Savior and my God."

-Psalms 43:5- (BSB)

Morning came quickly and Lilly found herself exhausted from thinking, unable to yield to her need
to gain a sense of direction. Finally, the thought
of numbness came to her. By numbing her memories, maybe she would be able to focus her thoughts
on the life that was still going on outside of the
abusive circumstances. She thought perhaps another strong drink would numb her, but it would
be counter-productive to any progress she needed
to make. How could she regain strength enough to
not be such a trifling mess? Lilly had casted her
cares to the Lord, but where was He? What could
He do to make either the pain subside, or make it
disappear? What could He do to make the burdens

that overwhelmed her lighter? How could she find rest in her current situation? She questioned His promises hopelessly. All of this seemed impossible. A Savior seemed like the knight in shining armor character found in a fairytale story: A tale of old or a dream that would never come true? Not this time.

As Lilly laid still restless and exhausted, suddenly a beam of light zoomed across the room. The intensity of its brightness made her tear up and squinch. She closed her eyes and repositioned herself to see more comfortably. As the beam still shone bright through her squinting lids, Lilly saw what appeared to be a straight blue horizontal line against a pixel golden background. As she focused in, the line turned into a body of water, and the golden background gathered up into an undefined human like figure. Glowing and growing, it appeared to be coming closer towards her. She was struck with fear, paralyzed at how real this sudden experience was becoming. How could she have doubted the Almighty God? What would He do to chastise her? Lilly was certain it would be worse than all the pain and anguish she was feeling just moments ago. She regretted being able to feel anything because it all felt like impending doom. Suddenly, her senses began to bring revelation. A warmth came over her as the beam of light glowed at an angle across her face, soothing her right side. The warmth slowly spread, encompassing her left side as well. She heard a still voice speak saying,

"Fear me not but put on my armor so that you may stand."

She squeezed her eyelids tightly together as the vision faded. Lilly became overwhelmed with transient exhaustion that transformed into a divine sense of peace. She quickly fell into a deep slumber. He had come in that moment not to judge, but to give her rest.

CHAPTER VI

Behold: A New Thing

"If I rise on the wings of the dawn, if I settle
by the farthest sea, even there your hand will
guide me; Your right hand will hold me fast."

- Psalms 139:9-10- (BSB)

In a few more hours, Lilly would be moving further north to begin life over. She would miss waking up to the lake view every morning and having coffee on the back patio. She would also miss her huge hidden office that set far back in the corner of the college library. Entering that quiet place had become a daily routine. Even when things got busy with new patrons, testing, and visits from the child development program, it was still quiet. She hoped that in her time there, her service had been a true help.

She missed her church family. Even though she had isolated herself for a while, there was always the opportunity to return right back on the scene. Now that Lilly was moving, this wouldn't be a practical option anymore. If she decided to return now, she would be welcomed back with overwhelming compassion, and consumed with the sincere love of all her sisters, but there was no desire to feel pitied. She knew there would be many questions but dreaded even more would be the sincere attempts to assist in a reconciliation that was now forbidden by law. While the move would help her dodge the uncomfortable feelings of dealing with her failed marriage, she would miss her church family all the same.

Lilly's marriage had been dissolved. Her thoughts drifted back to that life changing day. She had only expected to dangle the divorce in Oliver's face as a final ploy to convince him to seek help for his addictions. She failed. It amazed her how so much damage had been done: a criminal record ½ inch thick with photos of blackened eyes, two at a time; visuals of her battered face and arms; bloody hands and lips, and trauma filled images of her emotional pain. What started for Oliver as simple misdemeanor battery charges, eventually grew to domestic cruelty felonies. All of this, and still he remained in denial that there was a problem, a demonic disease. Had Lilly known that the compilation of so much evidence would be bond together and visible all at once, she would have saved herself the shame that came with being so forgiving of it all. She could not be forced to testify against him, and there was no doubt about that. The problem was, he knew this as well.

Lilly expected Oliver to show up to the divorce proceedings to fight for her; for them; just like she was willing to do. There was a glimpse of hope she held deep in her heart. Maybe he would recognize that enough was enough. Maybe he would finally choose her, and for once, shoot down the elephant that caused their tumultuous relationship. All this time, he had been oblivious to her pain, but maybe now Oliver could feel the pain he was inflicting on himself. He had finally comprised his freedom. There was no bailing out on this road. In her mind, he would show up realizing what he had to do his time. Hopefully, he would do so with the intent of coming out a better husband: a sober husband.

Even though blaming Lilly was a common theme in all things that went bad, that wasn't her expectation in these proceedings. Nevertheless, this was still the case. Oliver blamed her for not being able to reverse the sentence. Even though he was fully aware that it was out of her hands, he still blamed her. The difference this time was the desperation in his behavior. His blame was masked by phony apologetic efforts to persuade her to be his ally. He convinced himself that he had done nothing horrific, despite overwhelming evidence, despite witnesses, and despite other victims. Somehow, Oliver was sure that by acting more ashamed, remorseful, and regretful, he could convince her too. This time, he needed her help more than ever. This time, the situation was more dire than ever. This time, he was facing four years minimum with no chance of probation. Rehabilitation would not reduce the sentence; it would only be a part of it. Oliver was aware that he would be prosecuted to the fullest extent of the law, and her silence along with the other victims in the case meant nothing. The state would come after him with no holds barred! He would make the perfect example for junior domestic violence offenders, and he would cease to continue his reckless behavior once and for all. The court officers rallied to be sure of it.

Lilly's meek, humble, and forgiving nature did not help him as it had done in the beginning. On the contrary, it doomed him. In the eyes of the law, it was dangerous for her to continue to show him that kind of mercy. She was forced to realize it while sitting across from the judge expecting Oliver to appear. After waiting an hour past the original proceeding time, everything she had prayerfully expected to happen stumped her.

He did not come requesting to save their marriage. What was the point? It wouldn't grant him his prioritized freedom. This was the only proceeding 'O' wanted to participate in. Everything else was an aside. The one person he thought would be able to help had failed him. She had become useless. If Oliver had to sacrifice his freedom, he would abandon her as well.

Lilly could not believe it. She held on to what Oliver had said over and over; he would never divorce her, and he would never allow her to divorce him. She believed that with all her heart, but he proved her wrong. Crushed and desperate to salvage some portion of the relationship, Lilly recalled making a final plea to save him. An attempt to convince the judge that she wanted him to get the help he needed; that was her play. She could use her tenderness and mercy to win the judge over on his behalf. If Lilly could expose her husband's 'disease,' maybe he could get the medical, and psychological attention that was long overdue.

Ten minutes into the hearing, she made her move.

"Your honor, is there any way you can just make him do rehabilitation

without jail time? He is sick and he needs help. Incarceration is not the

answer here your honor. He is suffering with a genetic disease."

The judge dropped her chin and peered over her glasses. Pitifully confused by this victimized, battered, entrapped young woman, she replied,

"Have you seen this file?"

The judge tossed the thick bound manila folder across the table.

"Open it," she murmured.

Lily opened the folder to photos she had never seen before. Shockingly, each picture brought back the horrible memory of every incident. The judge continued.

"He can certainly undergo a rehabilitation program, but he will not be

excused from doing the time for these crimes. Sweetheart, you are a

victim. These incidents have occurred repeatedly over the course of five

years. Sorry to say it, but your blood will not be on my hands. The 'No

contact' clause stands indefinitely. I remember this man at the

arraignment with his slick talk, trying to get himself out of all the trouble

he had gotten into. Today is your lucky day young lady. I am going to

grant you this divorce. I am also going to see to it that this man serves sufficient time for doing this to you. It's the only way he's going to

realize that he cannot continue this type of behavior. If it isn't you, it is

going to be someone else. Listen to me carefully Lilly. You are young

with your whole life still ahead. Move on to something better. I see it in

you. You deserve better."

The judge signed the paperwork and put it in a folder.

"I'm sorry about the wait, but I tried to see if there was a delay in

escorting Mr. Oliver from the county jail. I do not like to divorce people

unless I hear both sides, but in your case, I've heard enough. Come with

me."

They stepped outside of the conference room into the main hallway. The judge summoned a court bailiff. She handed him the folder and instructs him to take it to the clerk's office. "Just follow him. Good luck to you dear."

This was not at all the outcome Lilly had expected, but nevertheless, it was final. The ink dried instantly. As the clerk finalized the decree, she tried to grasp what had just happened. Just like that, her marriage was over. Was it really? For now, it was. She was sure that he would somehow find his way back to her. He always did.

Drifting out of that painful past felt like a gut punch. Lilly gathered herself and finished packing all that she would take with her; mostly wall décor, clothes, photographs, and important paperwork. She had given most of her treasured kitchen belongings to her mother. The heavy red and gold Dutch ovens; the holiday dish sets that she loved so much; the stainless-steel pots and pans with matching lids; the upright stocked deep freezer. She had thrown in a vacuum and a carpet shampooer as well. The furniture in the living and dining room had been purchased by 'O.' Lilly had no desire to overload with useless items, so she donated the furnishings to a missionary thrift store. They came twice with a medium size truck and loaded all that was in the dining room and living room as well as a few beds, a futon, and a couple of dressers. All that remained was storage containers in the laundry area with Oliver's belongings; photo albums, seasonal clothing, a music collection, Italian suites, and a few leather attaché cases with important documents. She packed two suitcases, took them to his mother's house, and tasked her cousin with delivering all that was left for a few bucks. Everything else was loaded into large black lawn bags and taken to the curb for trash collection. The house was finally emptied and cleaned out within a few hours.

Lilly had expected to be on the road no later than 11a.m. It was about a 3-hour drive with only her puppy in tow for company. 'O' gave the puppy to her as a birthday gift the year before. At the time, she would have preferred clothing or jewelry, but the dog grew on her. It was a jet-black female Maltese Yorkie mix. She was cute, and quite social with plenty of personality. The two of them would adjust to their new start together and that was comforting.

All the things she had decided to take barely fit into the trunk and back seat of the white sedan. Lilly placed her jewelry boxes in a small basket on the front seat. That left just enough space for the puppy to rest by the basket or stretch out on the floorboard. A last-minute check was made to be sure the house was clean, and nothing was forgotten. She locked up and placed her keys in an envelope with a note containing the new address to be drop off at the landlords on her way out. With her last bittersweet goodbyes, the puppy relieved herself one final time. It was 11:15 a.m. so, she was right on schedule. Lilly hopped into the packed car and rode off, relieved to leave the old in the past.

She was excited to experience a new beginning, but also wished she had more insight on what to expect. There was no long-term plan at this point other than to seek God wholeheartedly and finish her degree. Surprisingly, her expectations were somewhat empty. She suspected it was because for once, she would finally be living lightly. Lilly had no idea that God had brought her out of enslavement and was about to send her into the wilderness for a season of renewal. She was totally unaware that her love for Him was about to grow to new heights. Now that she was stripped of all distractions, and stripped of Satan's mighty grip on her life, God would begin to show her His love in abundance. Little did she know that the grace He gave in allowing her to escape all the pain, was merely the beginning of a brand-new salvation. The mercy He had shown her for ignoring Him in so many situations, would now usher in an agape love that would overwhelm her forevermore. God would love her Himself with more love than she had ever known.

CHAPTER VII

Uprooted & Grounded

But ask the beast, and they will teach you; the birds
of the heavens, and they will tell you; or the bushes
of the earth and they will teach you; and the fish of
the sea will declare to you. Who among all these does
not know that the hand of the Lord has done this?

- Job 12: 7-9- (BSB)

Lilly opened her eyes to see the breaking of dawn
through the large unfamiliar window of her new
apartment. Across the high roof tops a few miles
off, there laid a beautiful landscape of hills, full of
vibrant life. All was silent except for the chirping
repetitious verse of a songbird. She listened closely
to time the rhythm of the song. Unable to distin-
guish when the verse would begin again, Lilly realized the uniqueness of God's wonderous creation.
All things were different, distinct in character and
function. She wondered about the song's message.
With equivalent patterns each time the verse was

chirped, she was sure it had a meaning. Was it a song of love? Was it a calling to the creature's mate or a testimonial to its Creator?

In the midst of these new surroundings, Lilly laid there taking in her new environment. There was more height in this place than she was used to. The ceiling was at least 8 feet taller than the bed level. The cavernous room seemed to consume her, and she felt so small in it. The walls appeared bright even in the faint light of day that slowly emerged from the hill's cape not far off.

She took in a deep breath and suddenly realized how faint and light her heartbeat felt. Exhaling, Lilly consciously paused to re-examine her sudden recognition of a feeling that had been within her all along; a feeling she never acknowledged, yet she *knew* it was there. Deep in between her eyes, a captivating pressure arose; a slight aching that was almost equivalent to the dull thumping heart she had allowed to go unnoticed all this time. Bound in a motionless trance, she was uncertain of where this perplexing feeling originated. Lilly laid so still that the vague thumping could be felt in her every limb. A deep aching warmth began to penetrate her chest just beneath the surface of her breast. Down into the scapula, a congested heaviness built; a weight she had been carrying all along but never realized. This heaviness had been buried within for as long as she could remember; present, but ignored, neglected, and omitted from her sense of being. Lilly continued to breath in a slow cadence, aware of how faint the beating of her heart really was. The dull ache had been there for so long, it had become normal; but now, it could be felt. She wondered if it had ever been different. Aside from the heart-throb of vigorous exercise in her youth, she could not identify any other recognizable cardio pattern. Then again, Lilly had never given it enough attention to recognize her familiar acquaintance with this warm pain. Until now, there was never an awareness that she had been living with heartache all along.

The tension between her eyes brought memories of the times she had cried; the times when she had been overwhelmed with emotional pain that buried this real living heartache inside of her. Lilly drew in breaths that were longer and deeper to be certain that what she felt was real. It was indeed a faintly beating, aching heart. As she breathed deeper, bypassing strong nasal tension and fostered tears, she could feel her heart's rhythm fade almost completely. Pausing in between her deep breaths to re-examine this revelation, she would take the time now to feel it completely and nothing else.

Lilly allowed time, space, and motionlessness to incarcerate her being for hours. Now conscious of her spiritual death inside for so long, only the shallow breaths kept her from an actual physical death. She stared beyond the ceiling as it faded away and slowly opened into a porthole of a bright sky. Holding her breath to see how close she was to death; Lilly began to levitate toward this beautiful skylight.

Gradually, her visibility was completely taken by a light so bright, it appeared to be golden. The warm feeling in her chest grew more intense as she drifted upward. What could be likened to a dim glowing candle wick now had the momentum of a spreading forest fire. Just as it was too much to bear, it rushed from her. The burning flowed from her chest to become one with the light that umbrellaed her. She was more capable of enduring it externally. The sensation completely shifted from heaviness to comfortability. In the intense warmth of the light, Lilly let go of all she could feel! Suddenly her being fell back into the body she briefly left behind.

She gasped for breath just as an instant hiccup stopped her heartbeat altogether. Just then, as her vision returned, the faint beating resumed. The dull deep burn presented itself once more, as she realized it had been with her all along. It had never left her and had never been altered. With another hiccup, her heart stopped again bringing confirmation of the congested heaviness she had carried this far in time. It remained and would be unchanged for now.

Still captured in the stillness that had just brought acknowledgement to her true condition, Lilly knew that she would have to continue operating subconsciously just as she had been doing for so long. How could she have been so fully functional in this broken condition? How could she have been so close to death while still living? No science or logic could explain it. The feeling was so close to lifelessness, she could only describe it as supernatural or miraculous; the greatest juxtaposition anyone could have ever known.

She slowly shifted her numb limbs. Lilly knew she had been able to function prior to this awe-inspiring epiphany, but this new knowledge birthed doubt that she would be able to continue. How could it be possible?

Suddenly the songbird began its verse again. There was no description for the sudden wisdom that gave life to the song's meaning. She knew the notes and why those very notes whistled with purpose and glory. Lilly could identify its timing with perfection. Her understanding was of a different time and place, heavenly and complete. Human language could not interpret the understanding she was given in that moment.

She came forth from the bed where her body laid almost lifeless for hours. Lilly had been only spirit in action for so long that she had not realized it. The activities of her limbs had nothing to do with the blood that flowed through her veins. It was only the spirit that flowed through those veins that keep her in motion. The same spirit that understood the song of the bird while she could not explain it in words. It made her stand to her feet. Still aware of the near still pulse within her, she stood anyway. Stretching her hands over her head, Lilly became one with the golden light that moments ago cascaded over her. She was living while not living at all, completely overjoyed by the mystery of it all; overwhelmed with thanksgiving and peace just as still as her heartbeat; fully aware that she had been carried this far by God's Spirit. Her praise would now be more glorious than the song whistled by the bird, expressed in a tongue too foreign for her ears to understand. The Spirit, however, would know every utterance. Her love for Him suddenly became larger than life! Lilly's awareness of this love became as miraculous as living without breathing or existing without a heartbeat. She would be forever different; consumed by a purpose she was completely unaware of in the natural. There was no doubt that her purpose would be fulfilled fluently, effortlessly, and naturally. The Spirit that had lifted her, would become her. The love of that Spirit would consume Lilly's very existence. Alive and in action, living by God's Spirit alone. Love so alive, that the biological flesh it was wrapped in would depend on that love for the rest of her life.

I ask that out of the riches of His glory He may strengthen you with power through His Spirit in your inner being, so that Christ may dwell in your hearts through faith. Then you, being rooted and grounded in love will have power together with all the saint, to comprehend the length and width and height and depth of the love of Christ, and to know this love that surpasses knowledge, that you may be filled with all the fullness of God.

- Ephesians 3: 16-19- (BSB)

CHAPTER VIII

Periwinkle Rag

But the Advocate, the Holy Spirit, whom the Father
will send in My name, will teach you all things and
will remind you of everything I have told you.

- John 14:26 (BSB) –

Lilly got up from the bed feeling refreshed with a
new sense of joy, and a new purpose for existing.
She started her chores with a smile in her heart.
They were things that didn't require much thought
because they had always been routine to her, washing laundry, doing the dishes, walking the dog. As
the chores progressed, she began to deeply reflect
on her early experiences in coming to know Christ.
Lilly was immediately reminded of her Grandmother Helena, and her powerful, easy, attractive
influence. She was strong but not overbearing, and
always full of humility. Her character was difficult
to want to duplicate yet easy to admire. Filled with

grace and thanksgiving, her personality spilled over into her charity. She was a steadfast woman, dedicated in her faith, and stern in obedience. Lilly reflected on her memories as a little girl; vivid memories that were hidden deep within her suddenly emerged:

> Grandma always rose before the sun early Sunday morning. She remembered drifting in and out of a doze, first jerked by the clicking of the light switch, and then the intense aroma of slow roasting sausage, onions, and bell peppers. Lilly would watch her standing in the mirror while she combed her long shiny locks. Inside of her grandmother's beautiful green eyes, she could see compassion and confidence, but most of all piety. It assured her that while in Helena's presence, there was an unseen power that would always provide protection. It sometimes felt eerie to be amid such a soft, meek, and humble spirit, often frequented by an opposingly fierce power. Lilly did not understand the source of this power, but it kept grandma virtuous, saintly, and upright always.
>
> She was sacrificial, never worrying about her own needs or wants. Besides the two simple skirts and blouses and the crisp white suit that she alternated on communion Sundays, she had no fine clothing; just a few house rags, one

torn in the collar, another lopsided on her hips from the failing old elastic. Grandma always compensated in fashion with the dressing of her hair, fashioning her curls with only oil, water, and a brush.

She found pleasure in perfecting simply things; a home cooked Holiday feast that was almost always too beautiful to eat; the landscaping of her yard adorned with ornamental grasses and mossed over slopes. Her annual and perennial beds were timed and planted perfectly for bloom. She was careful about everything she put her hands to. The stitching in the clothing she mended often looked better than the garment itself. It was difficult to find flaw in even her words; always spoken with passion, proper, and befitting of one who loved God and was adored by Him in return. This Godly intimacy that she owned, was magnetic to others. Everyone wanted to be within her reach, knowing that in her midst there was a true presence of a humble, yet almighty power. The five-bedroom home that she kept tidy, and comfortably decorated was full of loved ones needing to be close. Always a house full, including her mother, her children, their children, her sisters, and brothers; even distant uncles from out of state would wander in every now and again to enjoy the comforts of her home. She had the ability to force peace in every tense situation, making the bickerers ashamed to even think of contending inside of her ever-present pacifism. She was Shalom.

To leave her was to separate from a staggering power that encompassed consistent obedience and righteousness. When Lilly would wander from her grandmother's physical presence, wordless chastisement would often come by consciousness of her steadfast ways. She was the epitome of the Proverb 31 woman. Although Helena was without husband, she continued to be led by her one true love: Jesus.

Lilly recalled holding her hand entering the sanctuary. Her grandmother looked down at her, as she gazed upward focused on that beautiful smile. Ms. Helena sat Lilly upon her lap and adjusted her dress collar. Just as the preacher began to speak, she asked,

"Grandma, will you make more of the fry cakes with the special

jelly for me?"

Basking in these memories, she could still recall the scent of those buttery handmade biscuits covered in sticky sweetness. Immersed in the mundane chores of the day, her mental escape continued. She remembered grandma pressing her nose into her cheek and whispering,

"Hush baby, listen to the man of God."

Young Lilly wasn't quite sure of what that meant, but she knew that whatever the "man of God" had to say would be important to the people in the church. His sermon would always begin rhythmic and peaceful enough to doze off to. The little children were allowed to doze, but adolescents were encouraged to remain awake. The Pastor would start off with some sort of narrative, or a reading from the scriptures. He would gradually get the congregation's approval with a spontaneous response of, "Yes Elder", "Amen", or "Preach." All the children knew that they were to remain seated and quiet. Whenever the adults stood to clap, shout, wave, or praise, they knew their participation was only allowed during times of song. Even then, the youngsters were fearful of doing so not knowing what all the commotion was about. They only knew that giving absolute reverence to the adults and the boisterous on goings of each Sunday morning service was mandatory. The children were expected to sit still and remain quiet if the elders circled around a congregate who had fallen out or had begun to kick and shuffle around uncontrollably. Lilly recalled how the youngsters would look around at each other with a curious fear, knowing that anyone who breached their position would be chastised by the old female ushers dressed in white. What started out peaceful and harmonious always escalated into active participation of dancing, shouting, jumping, and praising. When the 'man of God' had finished bringing the 'Word of God', he would always ease the people into a closing of thanksgiving; just as he had begun, with a prayer. The members would all greet each other joyfully as they departed, reacquainting with congregates who had been absent for a while, and family that had traveled from afar to visit. She recalled sitting next to her grandma service after service, year after year. Gradually, her mysterious fear of the worship services shifted into a powerful reverence for the congregating of the people of God.

As Lilly got older, her family moved far away from Grandma and the Sunday morning traditions. Her mom got married and they drifted away to make a family of their own. They would travel on the bus for hours to visit Grandma during summers and Holidays, and Helena would always be overwhelmed with joy to welcome them back. She recalled being reluctant to give up that sacred place on grandma's lap to her baby sisters, but granny always kept a space at her side for Lilly to sit or stand. She was much too big by then to be a lap child, but that did not stop the steady flow of hugs and kisses. The constant yanking at some crooked, or untucked piece of clothing didn't stop either; always with that loving infectious smile Lilly missed so desperately.

Grandma and mom would talk about the usual: new recipes, the neighborhood, updates on family members, gardening secrets, and always baptism and salvation. It was obvious that mom would rather avoid the portions of the talk that emphasize the importance of a 'personal relationship with God', or 'keeping God first in her marriage.' Nonetheless, she was respectful; quietly agreeable and reverent.

Lilly recalled once asking her mother on their way back to the city about baptism: What did it mean? What did it do? She said that it was how we wash away all our wrongdoings, and become clean, new, and closer to God. In her mom's reluctance to explain at that moment, it terrified her. She wondered why mother had not gone through the process herself yet. Was she scared as well? More questions began to arise in Lilly's mind over the subject: What if the things her mother had done where so wrong that she was ashamed? Was God angry with her for those things? Was she hid-ing from God? The more she questioned her mom's state of unholiness, the more frightening the thought of becoming clean became. She pitied her mother and was very frightened for her. Lilly was frightened for herself even more. These memories and feelings were vivid! She recalled how dark it was on the bus that night. She felt uneasy watching her mother stare out the window in a blank gaze. Mother was deep inside of her own thoughts, recalling every sin, and every mistake. The reflection of her eyes could be seen in the bus window, bouncing back and forth as she anxiously switched from recollection to recollection. There was a troubling uneasiness and a panicked worry in her face. What started as fear in her youth and graduated to reverence in her adolescence, shifted to a terrifying fright. Lilly quickly dropped her head and peered into her own lap. She remembered how desperately she wanted to cry. To look into mother's eyes and see grandmother's strength would have been so reassuring in that moment, but fear and uncertainty were all that was present. Instead, Lilly looked at the side of her turned face, careful not to recapture her reflection in the window. Mother's expressions were still, and she breathed steadily. It was enough to calm her worried mind as she leaned on her mom's shoulder. It was enough to settle her until they reached their destination. Lilly envisioned her grandmother's reassuring eyes and a still calmness came over her as she drifted into a deep sleep for the remainder of the journey home.

"Peace I leave with you; My peace I give to you. I do not give to you as the world gives. Do not let your hearts be troubled; do not be afraid."

- John 14:27- (BSB)

CHAPTER IX

Down The Lane

"The fear of the Lord is the beginning of wisdom, and knowledge of the Holy One is understanding."

- Proverbs 9:10 - (BSB)

Lilly had finished the first load of clothes and dishes, and not even conscious of having done so until it was complete, prepped one of her grandmother's infamous Spanish rice recipes. She recalled grandmother being an amazing chef, preparing mass meals. She could measure ingredients by eye. She knew the perfect timing to produce the perfect texture in every one of her culinary creations, combining meats, herbs, and vegetables, in precise tempo. Her sense to pair ingredients was amazing, able to substitute variations of a bean, starch, or cut of meat to recreate a conventional dish with a fresh unique spin. Always welcoming to the senses.

Lily stepped back, and looked at what she had chopped, diced, washed, shredded, and rinsed to see if there was anything missing. To her surprise, she was able to recall every ingredient just as if she were her grandmother. The dog still needed to be walked, and it was a nice day to weed the yard if time permitted. She leashed her puppy, grabbed her comfortable sneakers and headed out. As she admired the beauty in nature. Coming from far behind her she saw the prettiest red cardinal fly ahead of her path and perch itself on a tree a few 100 feet ahead. Her great granny Darling would always say that red birds represented a relative that was no longer with us. As the bird seemed to wait for her to approach, her mind wondered. She drifted back into the old, but unexplored memories of her grandmother:

> She had left grandmother far behind at age 24, very timid, but noticeably confident as well. Lilly carried grandma Darling's wisdom along to ensure her character would reflect her stoic mentors in all she did, and in every word she spoke. Always striving to replicate her nature was no easy task. She never realized it would be so hard to even come close. In separation, they seldom kept in touch. Lilly missed not being physically present to see the reassurance in grandma's eyes when challenges arose. She desperately tried to convince herself that the

confidence was there; just hidden deep down inside.

Grandma Helena's summer cookouts were always special. She prepared the meals: potato salads, pasta salads, fresh sweet corn, homemade baked beans, banana puddings, fruity gelatin desserts, and perfectly seasoned meat to be grilled. They had a large family, so she would spend night and day preparing; humming gospel as she stirred and chopped, checked, and sampled. All her brothers and sons would assist with preparing the grill and trimming the lawn, all while sipping cold alcoholic beverages. They knew to smoke their cigarettes outside and not to litter the yard with the butts. Everyone was familiar with the shrewd look grandmother would give if they were out of order in anyway. She knew they would indulge in their pleasures, but it did not affect her behavior in the least. Out of respect for her faith, and love for the Lord they would play mild music like War, and Earth, Wind, and Fire. These were family favorites. She would come sit on the back porch for a little while once she had finished all the hard work. Grandma loved to watch the men play horseshoes, and the girls would jump rope or perform stunts on the swings. She would always panic when Uncle Joe suggested taking the kids for a spin on the motorcycle. Eventually, she would always submit to us having fun, but we had to wear a helmet and couldn't go further than the end of the road. Usually when everyone had gone for a ride and all her grandchildren were safe and sound, grandma would turn in for the night. She would occasionally peek out of the upper room window and watch my uncles spin and twirl us around as we danced into the night. Every once and a while someone with a bit too much alcohol in them would start an argument. Grandma would come and shut the party down or separate the troublemaker with a squealing threat to call the police. Sometimes the party ended, sometimes it didn't. Most of the time it didn't. Everyone would usually become sober enough to give her the reverence she deserved with little resistance. Her presence always seemed to set things right. She carried peace on one shoulder and love on the other.

Lily smiled as she recalled such precious memories from her youth. She longed to have just one more day, solely dedicated to getting to the core of what made her grandmother simultaneously the peace and power that she was. It was so mysterious to her. She pondered how gentle and caring this woman was, yet so powerful in silence. Her family honored her when she walked into a room. Away went the foul language, and the playful mockery that happened amongst close family when they got together. Every now and then, they could get her to join in with a subtle acquiescing taunt, but one they knew would allow her to ascend to her reverenced pedestal. All would cease in conversation much like when the judge enters a courtroom. She would usually follow up with a word of wisdom or even a directive, and then allow them to get back to business as usual, yet they did to genuflect before proceeding with their fun-filled shenanigans.

As Lilly recalled all of this, she was jolted by a critical memory that manifested in recollection for the very first time. It overtook her with emotional reminiscence: The day that she was saved.

CHAPTER X

Holy Sake

"In the last days, God says, I will pour out My Spirit on all people. Your sons and daughters will prophesy, your young men will see visions, and your old men will dream dreams."

- Acts 2:17- (NLT)

The flood of lost memories suddenly became as vivid and bright as the noon day sun. Lily's grandmother had taken a lengthy sabbatical from church attendance.   She still insisted the family attend, and Sunday morning routines were as if nothing at all changed except, she stayed behind.   Grandmother began a subtle disapproval of recent church affairs and gradually, as doctrine and routines began to change, she disconnected and left the congregation to their new and improved non-traditional Sunday morning services. Women, and young boys with spotty reputations began to assume pastoral roles. She would still engage in bible study at home, and frequently meet with the Elders, but she halted her Sunday appearances at the church altogether for an awfully long time. Lily was too young to understand. What grandmother made clear to her family was that they would continue to participate and appear in services, and there would be no compromising. Those of her children who were burdened with lugging their newborn infants now had the option of leaving them behind with her to solidify their expected attendance.

Lily was left to conclude that the reasoning for this was that grandmother knew her family still needed to grow in Christ. She was strong enough in her faith to remain in Christ without proximity to the body, and because this is rare, her wisdom drove her to demand her family's continuous presence amongst the congregation. Even though she disapproved of the shift away from traditional ways of the church, she knew that the Lord would remain present in His house, and the seeds that were necessary for her family's spiritual growth would be sown for a future harvest. Grandma remained adamant in her stance for righteousness and the ways of old which she believed would preserve the foundation for holiness. She could not get others to agree with her plight and therefore sanctified herself with the Word of God.

So, while Lilly was able to see the disassociation that her grandmother developed with the church, she still saw the importance of remaining in the church environment and continuously seeking God. Grandma never stopped laboring in prayer and rejoicing in praise. She watched her meditate daily in God's Word as she continued to live a holy life. In watching the ways of her grandmother, Lilly developed a firm fear of the Lord. She was not allowed to question grandmas disconnect, and those that had a full understanding dared not question it either. Grandmother needed no ally in maintaining her firm position. This would be her burden alone, for no one else was strong enough to bare this cross. They could not drink from this cup. Everyone else would continue to be fed spiritual milk like the babes they were.

Lily's fear of the Lord began to grow as she heard the Word preached, and as she saw God's grace and mercy manifest itself in her own life. She longed to know Him more in seeing his goodness. She wanted the same 'sweet communion' with Jesus that grandmother affectionately referred to. She was now cautious about sinful things once done without a second thought. It now dawned on her that God was watching. Lilly knew that she had done many things that the Lord disapproved of, and the fact that she was still alive to even recall these things was such a blessing. She began to understand mercy, for after all, death is the price we are supposed to pay for sin. Even with her short-comings, all her needs were met. This introduced her to grace, and faith in the sacrifice which was made for her to live through it all. Lilly began to long for the glorious eternity of salvation.   She couldn't wait much longer to surrender her life. The pleasures of youth began to frighten her into repentance.   How much longer would her life be spared? Had God not waited long enough? It was do or die.   She had been told about baptism and it was time for her to be washed and made new. Lilly felt that prolonging this would cost her everything. It was time to give up everything in exchange for eternal life. It was the best deal, and one that could not be delayed any further. She spoke with her aunt about baptism, and the arrangements were made hastily. The baptism would be done Saturday, October 31.

She remembered her grandmother being so pleased at the news. She hugged her tight and rocked her within the embrace. Lilly did not quite understand much of anything at this point. All she felt was a sense of urgency to go down into the water due to overwhelming fear. She imagined God being angry with her up until this point. Lilly felt that He would not be pleased until this was ac-complished, and until baptismal submersion, she would have to continue to tread with extreme caution. Up until this point, the Lord had extended way too much mercy, and she dared not ask for or expect anymore. She would finally be at ease once baptized and made new. God would love her in new purity, and no longer look down upon her. There would no longer be need for continuous pardons to no avail. She would have a second chance at being better, living better, and doing better with all her wrongdoing behind her. Lilly was anxious to have this relief and it was all that mattered.

It was finally baptism day and her mother, sister, and aunts arrived at the church early that Saturday afternoon. Some children were already out trick or treating. It was a cool morning as they all stood in front of the church waiting on the Elders to arrive. Lilly was nervous, and the palms of her hands were sweaty even in the brisk weather. They all headed up the stairs to gather in the lobby of the sanctuary. Lilly and her sister, who decided to be baptized as well, were given white gowns and towels. They were led into the bathroom to change, and their mother came in as well to keep track of all their belongings.

Finally, the Elders entered the lobby to greet the family, just as Lilly and her sister emerged from the restroom dressed for their washing of newness. Instead of entering the sanctuary of the church that they were familiar with, they were directed down an unfamiliar hallway, which led to a descending staircase. It was damp, cool, and a bit musty. They arrived in an unfamiliar room, and at the center was a large old concrete pool. The pool water was clear, but some blots of dirt covered the bottom. There were concrete stairs set inside that led form the ledge down to the center of the pool. As they all gathered in the room, the chief Elder began to pray. Lilly couldn't really focus on the prayer; she was too overwhelmed with relief for making it to this day, somehow arriving without encountering the deserved wrath of God for her former way of life. She was grateful that her sister decided to surrender as well. They were close and they could share this new life and journey together just like they did in the mischievous ways of their youth.

It was finally time. The Elder entered the pool first and stood on the ledge as he held his hand up and out to her. She placed her hand into his, and with the other hand, held the bottom of the long white baptismal gown. The water was cool. Lilly stepped in slowly, a bit tensed by the temperature. She was instructed to squat and hold her nose.

"In the name of the Father, the Son, and the Holy Ghost,"

and down she went. It was quick. She was guided back up the steps, out of the pool, and wrapped in towels as her sister stepped in for her turn. All she could feel was overwhelming gratitude and relief.

Nothing felt any different physically, but her faith made her feel forgiven, new, and refreshed. She was extremely thankful for an opportunity to start life over.

CHAPTER XI

Whispering Revelation

"Jesus said to her, "I am the resurrection and the
life. Whoever believes in Me will live, even though
he dies. And everyone who lives and believes
in Me will never die. Do you believe this?"

– John 11:25 – (BSB)

The next day in Sunday service, Lilly arrived anxious and nervous about something that she could
not quite identify. The service was being held in an
old country town elementary school auditorium.
The aura of the auditorium whispered history, not
quite the same as the damp church basement, but
history all the same. As she folded down the heavy
spring enforced auditorium seat, she sat down,
then lifted the wooden splintered desktop leaf that
was tucked next to the seat at her right. The place
had a musty old smell with its dry mill dust aroma
infused with old fashioned perfume. There was
also a thick robust scent of olive oil the pastor used

to anoint the heads of those he would pray for.

The small congregation was mixed with young, old, black, white, and a few native Americans. The pastor himself was West Indian with a thick accent. Lilly recalled times that she wasn't really interested in coming. After the general scripture was given and exegeted for the focal meat of the message, the remaining sermon was drowned out by a foreign emptiness that left her comprehension incomplete. It was difficult to grasp the message through the pastor's thick island accent. The older crowd seemed to be right in tune as they shouted and rejoiced with raised hands. Some would leap in place; others would surrender to their knees. Passionate tears and joy through worship were always present, and all she could do was observe with a wild curiosity. Lilly possessed an overwhelming desire to be able to understand it all and be a part of it all. Her ignorance made her timid, yet the unidentifiable power in the air planted a deep seed of faith within her. She longed to feel the passion she saw in others, whether joy, pain, or conviction.

Just as devotionals commenced, she turned around and saw her grandmother breach the elevated entrance at the rear of the auditorium. It shocked her! Her grandmother had not been amongst the congregation in an awfully long time. As she recalled, never to this elementary school auditorium. Since last attending, there had been a split in the congregation. Lilly remembered the last time she had sat in her grandmother's lap was back in the old sanctuary where she had just been baptized. It felt like a long time ago. She was in middle school back then, but now Lilly was a teen. Although much more mature, she still had the same childlike timidness amongst the congregation of saints.

She immediately wanted to be next to her grandmother, longing for the nurturing comfort that she used to find while sitting in her lap as a little girl. Lilly arose and turned to join her grandmother in the back of the large dim room, but her grandmother gestured with her hands that Lilly should remain just where she was. She obeyed and sat back down.

As devotion began, maintaining focus was difficult, and her participation was dull and ingenuine. She was shocked that grandma would appear amongst the congregation after all these years. Her separation from the body was due to a disagreement in allowing women to take certain positions. Based on her biblical teaching and understanding, grandmother was adamant in her stance. Lilly recalled overhearing her grandmother's side of the argument.

"A woman has no place preaching or teaching, and that's the Word of

God."

She would not be moved. As long as the church continued the practice of allowing women to serve as deacons, or pastors, she would separate herself. She recalled her grandmother's fear of adapting to new ways, and her determination to follow what she believed to be right. Grandma was still the same loving, prayerful, faithful, god-fearing woman. She just refused to go with the new norms.

Lilly questioned deeply during praise and worship,

"Why is she here? What made her change her mind?"

She looked back to see if the answers could be found within her grandma's eyes, much like she could find the comfort and reassurance she often sought. All she could see was the back of her grandmother's head as she kneeled in silent prayer, rocking gently. The mystery over grandmother's presence disrupted her ability to receive the spiritual message of the sermon. Usually, Lilly could cut through the Pastor's thick Trinidadian accent to understand the jest of what was being preached before the Holy Spirit fell. After that, everything spoken whether in tongues or in broken English became a blur. She was overwhelmed by her what's and why's as it related to this unexpected mysterious appearance of her dear grandmother.

When the service settled down, and the rejoicing, dancing, shouting, and jumping ended, grandmother tapped her on her left shoulder. The familiar hint of Grandma's signature scent, Este Lauder's Youth Dew, settled Lilly's curiosity for a moment with that sweet comforting aroma. She spoke only,

"Don't be afraid. God is with you."

After kissing Lilly quickly on the cheek, she then turned, hugged a few familiar members, and scurried out the back auditorium entrance.

It happened to be Halloween, and it was a brisk damp Autumn Day. As Lilly stepped outside of the old schoolhouse, her eyes were captivated by the vivid colors of the falling tree foliage. She couldn't help but admire the scenery as they drove down the old narrow winding roads. Occasionally a home with webbed shrub surroundings or a porch decorated with Jack-O-Lanterns would appear. It all fit in with the season. Thanksgiving was just around the corner and Lilly loved it more than any other holiday. She was anxious to enjoy the large traditional family gathering. Distant uncles and other relatives would travel back home for this Holiday, so it was always full of fun and laughter: watching the adults engage in competitive card games like Spade and Bid Whist; singing and dancing to old favorites on the record player. Thanksgiving always brought a joyous family gathering, and the food was nothing short of amazing.

As they had gotten closer to their destination, Mother Marshall (the family called her Aunt Julia) began singing. She had a beautiful strong voice. It was always pleasant to hear her sing about the goodness of the Lord. When she talked about Him, there was a distinct sternness in her voice that expressed a corrective sort of chastisement. It was convicting and usually uncomfortable yet embarrassing: "Cover your head right now." Or "Stand when God's Word is being read." Sometimes it was just a forceful angry gesture to rise to your feet when the pastor entered the pulpit. So, to hear her express love for the Lord in song was always fulfilling. Lilly enjoyed singing along because Mother Marshall would always express a loving approval and adoration at the sound of her voice.

"Your voice was made to give God glory,"

she'd always compliment with delight. After a few verses and choruses, Mother Marshall said something strange.

"It is time to tarry for the Holy Spirit."

Lilly was unsure of what that meant but continued to hum the lingering melody with joy. She peered out of the window as they drove along while others in the vehicle had conversations about changing their destination. After a while, Lilly's Aunt Dee leaned over and whispered,

"We are going to Sister Angie's house."

The driver turned on some gospel music and they rode for quite a distance.

Upon parking at their final destination, they all emerged from the vehicle. It was a cool early afternoon. Lily felt a bit hungry and was unsure of why they were here. She began to revisit her curiosity for why grandmother decided to show up, and what she meant by 'Don't be afraid.' Thinking that they would simply fellowship or have an in-depth bible study, she didn't ponder too much about what was to come in the next few hours. Mother Marshall was always 'led by the Spirit,' so it wasn't uncommon to do things spontaneously. Sometimes, they would pull over at the drop of a hat so that she could evangelize to a stranger. Other times they would be at a nursing home praying for someone that had been mentioned on the "sick and shut-in list" at service. God's power was always present in her leading, so no one would ever dare object to her leading.

They ended up at a large newly built apartment complex; one could tell by the unfinished landscaping and ongoing construction. As they walked up a small flight of winding stairs, it began to drizzle, making it just in time to beat an oncoming down pour. As everyone entered this large apartment, the older saints immediately began to pray. Lilly nudged her Aunt Dee,

"What's going on?"

Her aunt replied,

"We're tarrying for the Holy Spirit."

Sister Angie's husband John anointed Lilly's head with his thumb and began to pray a prayer that she had never heard before. Suddenly, she was stricken with fear of an unfamiliar kind! As he cupped her head front and back with the palms of his hand, he began to tremble and said, "In the mighty name of Jesus, let your Holy Spirit fall on your child." Lilly became even more afraid as she stiffened her posture to stabilize her stance. The man began to tremble more violently, still gripping, but now slightly jerking her head. Suddenly, that robust oily scent in the auditorium emerged, this time interrupted by the scent of her grandmother's perfume. Then, grandma's face, like something in a dream flashed before her. "Don't be afraid, God is with you." She recalled her words and became overwhelmed with fear and an unexpected spiritual infiltration.

"The people walking in darkness have seen a great light; on those living in the land of the shadow of death a light has dawned. "

- Isaiah 9:2 – (BSB)

CHAPTER XII

The Upper Room Tarry

"Peace I leave with you; My peace I give to you. I do
not give to you as the world gives. Do not let your
hearts be troubled do not be afraid. You heard Me
say, 'I am going away, and I'm coming back to you."

– John 14:27 (NIV) -

Before long, everyone in the room was in worship,
prayer, and praise. Lilly was led to a sofa, where she
knelt. Mother Marshall took her scarf and placed it
over Lilly's head and shoulders. She sat at her side
as a coach giving simple instructions:

"Repeat the name of Jesus. Keep doing it:
Jesus, Jesus, Jesus, Jesus.

Keep going until your tongue is loosed, and
you'll begin to speak

whatever falls on your heart."

As simple as the instructions were, Lilly didn't comprehend the task at hand. Mother Marshall continued,

"Come on, Jesus, Jesus, Jesus, Jesus."

Lily labored in the task, not understanding what would change. After what seemed like at least an hour of just calling on the name of Jesus, she was weeping with weariness, and discouragement. Mother Marshall's stern instruction was frightening.

"You can! Keep going 'til you feel your tongue loosed"

Lilly closed her eyes. As she mustered up more breathe to continue crying out the name of the Lord, suddenly a rush of what felt like an inward wind pushed out of her mouth. She could feel the rush like warm air hitting the back of her teeth. And then utterance of a foreign language followed as she began to pour out what she felt within her. As she began to speak out in tongues with intensity, she came up onto her feet.

Lilly was possessed by a Spirit that made her dance and praise like never before. She surrendered control and continued rejoicing in a foreign utterance for what afterwards, seemed like hours. Constantly resisting the urge to control her words and actions, she finally resolved to a total surrender to the Spirit. It was a surrender that took her so far from herself, she would never be able to totally recall all that happened in those moments. Lilly was lost in a praise that celebrated salvation, forgiveness, and a relationship that would forever change her from that moment forward.

When she finally opened her eyes, she could see that it was beginning to get dark outside. As Lilly slowly came back to herself, it was clear that something had changed dramatically from within. She was overwhelmed with a rejoicing peace; a salvation that with all her effort, she could never attain before. It was a matter of finally surrendering to God's Spirit as she received his amazing gift.

In accepting Him, He became a part of her. Through the process, all uncleanliness was extracted. The slight aching of her head that she didn't realize existed until then, had gone from her. Lilly had been gifted with an adoption that made her new and childlike. She experienced a peace and relief like nothing she would ever experience again with that initial intensity. As the praising slowly subsided and this new peace settled amongst all present, an overwhelming feeling of exhaustion took hold. She slept the entire way home.

They pulled into her grandmother's driveway, and Lilly recognized the crackling gravel as her aunt nudged her awake. As she got out of the car and entered the house, her grandmother was sitting there in anticipation of what she already knew had happened. Her eyes widened with a confident smirk as her hands met each other in front of her. Aunt Dee affirmed with emphasis

"She got filled!"

Her grandmother nodded and smiled,

"Go get some rest,"

as if she knew exactly what she had encountered. Sleeping through the night was heavenly.

As she slept into the early afternoon, Lilly was awakened by an inward urge, a silent calling. She sat up and reached for her bible, not giving much thought to the happenings of the night prior. There was something she needed to know from God, and she didn't hesitate to attempt to find it. Lilly asked out loud,

"What's next Jesus?"

She opened her bible to Luke 21 and read the chapter in its entirety. The scripture gave her no revelation of what to do, or how to walk in her newness of life. She was looking for a bold instantaneous connection with the Lord, but there was nothing. Strangely enough, there was no desire to do any of the things she would normally do without a second thought. The urge to smoke was gone, and the urge to drink was gone as well. All the fleshly desires she once had were no more, yet there was no sense of direction.

Lilly got up and got dressed. Her mother and sister needed to run some errands, but neither had driver's licenses, so she was recruited to chauffeur the two around town. They usually drove around together, so it would be a normal day out, or so she thought. As they rode around town, it was typical for them to share a cigarette during the ride, only this time, Lilly had absolutely no desire to smoke. Her mother was sitting in the passenger's seat and passed her a cigarette. She refused it, so her mother put it out in the ash tray. They shopped and talked as they normally did. Her mother was comical by nature, so they always enjoyed shopping together. After leaving the grocery store, the three ladies headed towards City Hall to get a replacement birth certificate for her mom. Lilly's mother lit another cigarette for the ride and passed it to her. Suddenly, as she pulled out of the shopping plaza and reached for the cigarette, a vehicle appeared out of nowhere almost hitting the passenger side of the car where her mother sat! It shook all three of them up badly as the mysterious driver held down his horn in rage. As she continued driving, still in a state of shock, Lilly inquired,

"Mom, did you see where he came from?"

"No,"

her mother replied holding her chest as she took a long drag of the cigarette. She attempted to pass it over to Lilly, but she sharply refused considering what had just happened. Her sister attempting to bring humor to the situation from the back seat jumped in as she reached for the cigarette,

"Dang, maybe me or mom should drive." They all laughed.

After stopping at a drive through for lunch, the girls headed to the City Hall. It wasn't too crowded, so they were done in about 30 minutes. Heading back to the car, Lilly's mother said,

"I'm sitting in the back, this time, and thank God I'm wearing a maxi

pad, or I would've pissed the seat up."

They all laughed recalling the unexpected driver from earlier.

Her sister chimed in,

"Yeah, I'm gonna be chain smoking for the rest of the day, my nerves

are so bad now."

Lily chuckled and replied,

"Shut up and put your seat belt on,"

as her sister reached to push in the lighter for her cigarette. Lily looked both ways and just as she was pulling out of the parking lot, another mysterious vehicle came inches from hitting their car on the passenger side! Her sister let out quite a few fowl words, then shouted,

"That's it, I'm driving pissy and all."

Her mother clowned sarcastically by grabbing the exit handle on the car top. Lilly inquired once again,

"Did you all see him coming?"

Her sister snapped back,

"You obviously didn't see him coming four eyes."

She continued,

"If I've got to ride with you two, I'm better off walking home. Pull over!

I'll see y'all when I get there."

"Oh, girl hush," Lily responded.

They made it back to the house and gathered to watch their usual game shows while grandma cooked dinner. Although everyone got news about Lilly's experience the night before, no one treated her any differently. They didn't ask questions or say anything unusual. It was family time, and the evening went on as if nothing had changed, but Lilly had changed, and she knew it. She felt different but didn't know how to act different outside of avoiding sinful behavior. When she walked into the kitchen, her grandmother was finishing up the meal and asked,

"How do you feel?"

"I feel okay," She replied.

"I know you were tired when you got in last night.

We call that getting slain in the Spirit."

Lilly suddenly became curious.

"Do I look different, grandma?"

"No," her grandmother replied.

"You should feel a little different though. Delivered from somethings?"

Lilly replied,

"Yeah, kinda. I don't want to smoke anymore. I guess you can say I feel

sorta new."

"Ah hah, that sounds about right," her grandmother reaffirmed.

"Get into the Word, day and night. God's got

much to say, and that's

how you begin to hear Him baby."

Lilly enjoyed dinner with the family, and after cleaning up, she retreated to the room where she slept while visiting her grandmother. It would be time to leave soon, but she was glad to have been able to spend a long weekend with the family. Thanksgiving was right around the corner so it would not be long before she would return. Lilly got into her pajamas and sat down on the bed. Remembering what her grandmother said, she picked up her bible and revisited the bookmarked scripture she had read earlier that morning. As she meditated on the chapter and recalled the events of the day, a verse leaped out to her! Luke 21:15-16 read:

"For I will give you speech and wisdom that none of your adversaries

will be able to contradict. You will be betrayed even by parents, and

brothers and relatives, and friend and some of you will be put to death."

All she could think of was telling her mother no to the cigarette and the double near- death experience with both her mother and sister in car. Lilly was in awe. She said aloud, "Jesus, you really do speak through your Word." This was the first of many times she would hear clearly from God, through His

Word.

> "But the Advocate, the Holy Spirit,
> whom the Father will send in My name,
> will teach you all things and will remind
> you of everything I have told you. And now
> I have told you before it happens, so that
> when it does happen, you will believe."
>
> -John 14:26,29 – (BSB)

CHAPTER XIII

Tender Heart

"Just as you who formerly disobeyed God have now received mercy through their disobedience, so they too have now disobeyed, in order that they too may now receive mercy through the mercy shown to you. For God has consigned everyone to disobedience so that He may have mercy on everyone."

- Romans 11:30-32 – (BSB)

Lilly was 29 years old. She had already experienced far too many failed relationships with men. Always giving her full commitment to some guy that had no holding foundation in God and had no intent on doing right by her; at least not in the context of what was biblically correct. She found herself in relationships that lasted for years in hopes of a long-term marital commitment that none of her beaus seemed to be interested in. After 10 years in the last relationship, with a candid refusal of commitment in marriage, Lilly finally wanted her independence.

She felt so unequally yoked in lowering her moral standards for a time that she thought would only be temporary. She had linked up with an older gentleman, financially stable, set in his ways, yet satisfied with living life as they had done it for the last 10 years; in what he called commitment, and she called sin. Lilly was left with an unsatisfied 'longing to belong' after having done all that was required of a good wife: Cooking, cleaning, assisting in his business affairs, all while establishing her own business. She finally asked about the direction of the relationship only to be told that it was fine in its current state. At that point she was far from her family, but still longed to have the grand ceremony of a wedding that young girls dream about. Lilly was sadly disappointed and really didn't know how to digest another failure. Wasting the last 10 years of her life and not being placed on the pedestal of honor that she truly deserved was a tough pill to swallow. After months of inconspicuous suggesting turned to subtle nagging, he finally told her,

"You are my wife. Do you know what common law is bitch?

Leave it alone already."

That was her breaking point. She knew that she

would leave, and with all they had accumulated together over 10 years, it wouldn't be easy. Deep in her soul, there was a call to be regarded higher; a gnaw that tugged on her inner desire to be loved deeply. Lilly wasn't an average woman. She took great care in keeping herself well groomed, and maintaining a beautifully decorated, clean, and comfortable home. She prepared homestyle meals daily, all while assisting him in building his business, and advancing her own career. She was meticulous in her care for this man: buying him designer outfits, and handsome colognes for the few times he had agreed to take her out. Most of the time, they would sit and watch the news and have in depth conversations about politics or watch sports over a few beers. Sometimes, they would have cookouts and invite their neighbors and a few friends. It was a laid-back settled life, but Lilly wasn't settled in her heart.

She lost a lot of her possessions in the separation, but she gained a sense of newness knowing that she would be that much closer to right standing with the God that she had ignored for far too long. Her life before the breakup wasn't horrible. It was just in a strange way, incomplete: lacking the honor and praise that the Father was worthy of, and the relational dignity that she'd worked so hard to experience. Subconsciously, she was longing for the love only God could give, but gradual depression would lead her in the opposite direction of the light into a pitch-black darkness. All the fowl things that could numb Lilly began to draw her further and further away, and in the midst of that darkness, she found him: Oliver.

He was a slender, tall, strong man. Oliver was handsome and well built, but his witty humor made him even more attractive. The match maker of boozed oblivion would introduce them to each other at this place called common disfunction. Both were unhealed from past wounds. Lilly wanted more than her past had given her, but for so long, she remained unaware that Oliver was stuck in his past. He was content with being numb for the remainder of his life, but being blinded by his charm, she couldn't see these glaring issues. The more she drifted into the dark, it became easier to look beyond the present pain of her life. It was far easier to conjure up a false future of happiness based on his inebriated agreeableness. He seemed to want a future much like the past she had forgotten. Oliver was sincerely interested in her company and companionship. He was lust wearing a mask of promise, belonging, happiness, fun: all things good. He even related to the idea of God being his personal anchor in a troublesome time, which automatically translated into "right direction" for her. Being lackadaisically open to the idea of getting closer to God, his compliance tactic was sure to present a path of low resistance in his sprint toward her surrendered femininity. The strategy was second nature to him, and undetectable to her having been so submerged in her vulnerable trust. Lilly's familiarity with companionship, and her longing to be irresistibly desired, overrode any red flag of disaster in the making.

Oliver's desire for Lilly came across as his top priority. After a few months of spending time together, he would send her home with his credit cards and freedom to buy anything she chose. She would buy nice things for him instead. Lilly was angelic: a being of hope that could possibly pull him out of the familiar darkness he had gotten comfortable in; the invisible bondage that unabatingly cloaked him like his own skin. She was beautiful, intelligent, and provocatively intriguing to him. Oliver showed admiration for her sense of business skills, often asking for help in composing agendas for his managerial meetings. He inconspicuously tested her mentally, and physically, always impressed by her stamina. The better she performed, the more responsibility he gave her. On paydays, he would call her to meet him on his lunch break. He would hand her significant amounts of cash, a list, and a stack of bills. Her name would always appear at the top of the list with a decent little growing allowance. This impressed her. He was diversely sexy and malleably suitable, strong enough in physical stature to present the desired allusion of protector and provider. Beyond Oliver's obvious flaws, she could easily fantasize an amazing future with this man; one filled with good times, laughter, sensuality, and romance. Lilly knew he was into her, and she gradually allowed him more and more access.

After transitioning out of her old home, she had been trying to prepare herself to move into a new place. Following the breakup, she temporarily moved in with one of her girlfriends from work. This was good at the time because Lilly needed the emotional support and wiggle room to increase her savings. As she and Oliver got more serious in their relationship, he would often invite her to stay with him. She wanted desperately to do things right, and he took an understanding stance each time she refused to move in.

It was early February: snow was in the forecast, and it was bitter cold. She had always been one to despise moving, especially after traveling so far from the north to begin a new life with her ex. The promise of snow intensified the dread of the moving process: finding a place, having to pack and drag her belongings out of storage, unpack, arrange things, and get settled in. Wherever she ended up, Lilly wanted this move to be permanent. At that thought she became motivated enough to press through the hustle of it all.

Just as she was preparing to head in for a short day of work at the office, Oliver texted her an unknown address, proceeded by

"Can you meet me here at around 3pm? I want you to meet a friend of mine." She'd have a free day to house hunt after she got her team settled, so she agreed.

Lilly had looked at a couple of townhomes, but she wasn't too thrilled about any of them, disheartened by either their location, price, or interior design. After grabbing a late on the go lunch, she parked at a gas station, grabbed a newspaper, and checked out the classifieds. As she ate and flipped through the paper, snow flurries began to swirl across the windshield. In the many years she had been in the south, snow had never fallen. She was reminded of how pretty it was back north and got excited about witnessing the familiar beauty of this uncommon treat. After circling a few prospect locations, making a few phone inquiries, and leaving a few messages, Lilly checked some online stats for work and noticed it was almost time to meet Oliver. She headed over to the address and admired the white blanket of snow that was gradually accumulating on the ground and tinted the tree branches.

Upon reaching the address, she parked and looked around. For some reason she was expecting to be at a commercial business because the street number was 600. It was a short street with only about 3 or 4 houses on each side. The one labeled 600 was a small well-kept ranch house on a large corner lot. It had a nice curb appeal with a huge pecan tree that shaded the small front porch. The lengthy driveway led up to a fence of high azalea hedges that hid the back yard. Across the street was another small ranch home, simple in design, but well-kept from the exterior. She liked the old-fashioned streetlamps that sat on each corner of the street in the front of the homes. Brushed with a layer of snow, they reminded her of a scene that resembled something out of the North Pole. The snow was thick enough to lightly cover the driveway, sidewalks, roof tops and hedges. She was alerted by an incoming text from Oliver that read:

"Pulling up in a few. Had to make a quick stop."

Lilly watched her windshield wipers brush symmetrically packed semicircles of snow at each upper corner of her windshield. She rolled down her window to cause the snow accumulating on her driver side window to avalanche to the ground. Just as she rolled the window back up, she got a glimpse of Oliver's car turning the corner and pulling up behind her in her. She was excited to see him, and he was smiling. He jumped out of the car and approached her pulling a long-stemmed red rose from behind his back.

"You're gonna love this."

Thinking that he was speaking of the rose, she said. "I do. Thank you."

"Where did this snow come from?" he continued.

He pulled his hood over his head and ran around the front of her car to hop into the passenger seat. Just as he closed the door, his phone rang. As he began a conversation with the caller, she admirably focused in to examine and smells her rose.

Oliver greeted the caller and listened in silence. He looked over to her smiling, but before he responded back to the caller, he reopened the car door to exit. He walked off toward the rear of the car, closing the car door. As he continued the conversation for a few minutes, she could see another car had pulled up behind his out of her rear-view mirror.

Oliver put his phone in his pocket and walked over to the car. A short middle-aged gentleman stepped out. They shook hands, exchanged a few words, and then walked up the driveway towards her. Oliver opened her door and reached for her hand as he began his introduction:

"Lilly, this is Allan, one of my coworkers at the plant. Allan, meet

Lilly."

Allan nodded and smiled.

"Very nice to meet you Mr. Allan," said Lilly.

"Likewise," Allan responded. "O tells me good things about you. Funny,

I've known this joker for years, but I can't think of anyone he brags

about like you, so this is a pleasure." They all laughed. Allan continued.

"O says you are looking for a house?"

She was completely thrown off by his question, expecting to be having lunch with one of O's high school buddies or the cousin that he'd recently mentioned would be coming into town that month.

"Actually, I am." She responded curiously.

"Well, this house here is owned by my niece, who lives quite far from

here. It was owned by my late brother who left it to her. Now because

she lives so far, I manage things for her. Want to take a look at it?"

She looked at O as he smiled and nodded with approval at the suggestion.

"Sure, why not?" she replied.

She and O followed Allan up the inclined driveway and to the front door. Allan wiped his snow trodden feet as he entered in and they followed suit, both noticing a light beige carpet first. The room was simple, like most unfurnished rooms would be. A few of the windows set high into the walls giving a sense of privacy and security.

They walked through the living room into a moderate sized kitchen that connected to a hallway leading to the remainder of the house. Lilly skimmed for potential: plenty of cabinet space; a window that looked out into the back yard, dishwasher, refrigerator, but no stove.

Looking down the hall to the remainder of the house, it looked much smaller than its actual size. She counted rooms as they checked out each one: four in all, plus one bathroom right off the hallway, and another half bath tucked in the corner of the master bedroom. It was far more spacious than its moderate appearance from the outside. The bathrooms were both saintly white. It was quaint and clean. Not as modern as she would have liked, but very spacious on the inside.

Back off into the kitchen was a laundry room, and a backdoor that led into the backyard. They stepped out onto a tin roof canopied deck, which she absolutely loved. Off to the right was a well-built storage house and another storage shed. She was a bit surprised at the additions, plus the back yard was huge. As she walked through, she noticed small little nooks and crannies with the potential to use as garden beds or discrete his and her patio settings.

Over on the left side of the yard behind the high azalea fence was so much space she was shocked. Lots of yard, with a sectioned off garden bed in the corner. The hedges were so high that you could not have guessed that much property sat behind them from the street.

As they rush back to the covered deck to escape the snow, Allan began to highlight the sellable commodities:

"The dishwasher has to be replaced, and you'll need to buy a stove of

course, and maintain the yard, but there is what we call a 'desirable

pecan' tree in the front. The nuts are huge. Over there in the front

corner by the lamp post, there's a peach tree. Yeah, so four bedrooms,

1 ½ baths $550 a month. $1500 is first month and security."

Her eyes got wide with amazement.

"You're kidding?" She interrogated.

"Rent to own, my niece is willing to let it go for $35 to $40 thousand.

She took her dad's passing pretty hard and it reminds her of him."

"I'm so sorry to hear about your loss, sir."

Lily extended her condolences as she sensed Allan's covered grief as well. Oliver nodded in agreement as he placed both hands on her shoulders. He was determined to lighten the air moving forward knowing his friend's pain over the loss.

"Well Lil, what do you think? That storage space over there would be

perfect to renovate into your own personal office. There is plenty of

room inside and the yard is amazing, isn't it?"

Oliver knew his convincing charm was on full display. Lilly smiled with delight. She was moved by how thoughtful, helpful, and romantic his surprise was. She couldn't refuse such a fantastic offer, so she agreed. They exchanged information and agreed to some final arrangements that evening if the weather held up. Allan locked the gate as they exited the backyard and waved as he headed out.

"We'll talk later O.," said Allen

"Thanks man, I appreciate it bro."

Oliver turned his total attention toward Lilly grabbing her into a big bear hug.

"Happy early Valentine's baby. I gotta run to take care of some stuff,

but make sure you give me a call when you get settled. Ok? I love you."

He kissed her softly and rubbed her cold hands as he broke down the driveway back to his car. She stood there and waved.

Though it was cold, the air was refreshing. She felt content, adored, and relieved all at once. She looked around once more to admire what she would in just a little while call home.

CHAPTER XIV

Deceived Heart

"For your husband is your Maker- the lord of Hosts is His name- the Holy One of Israel is your Redeemer; He is called the God of all the earth. For the Lord has called you back like a wife deserted and wounded in spirit like the rejected wife of one's youth says your God."

- Isaiah 54:5-6 - (BSB)

Oliver made the move easy for her. She rented a truck. He gathered his baby brother and a few of his friends and took care of just about everything; even most of the unpacking. He left her to arrange her belongings the way she wanted.

One of his buddies ran for pizza and beer as they finished unloading the truck with the remainder of her belongings from storage. The guys ate, and some grabbed slices to go as they wrapped up for the day.

As the evening grew on them, it was just she and O. She was very thankful and quite impressed for all he had done in the process. Lilly felt comfortable with allowing him to take the lead.

As he sat down at the bar height table in the kitchen, he grabbed for her hand pulling her closer in between his swaddled long legs. She stood in the middle of his straddle, and they were almost eye to eye in height.

"I'm exhausted." He confessed.

"I bet." she responded

"You really got it done, and fast. Thank you so much for everything."

"I can think of some ways you could really thank me,"

he teased as he softly pinched her jaw. He leaned in to kiss her. As he was reluctant to not get too deep into it, he slowly pulled back and gazed at her.

"You are incredible, and I need to go take a shower. Let me get going.

I'll come by tomorrow night after work to help rearrange the furniture in

the rooms."

"You can shower here," she offered.

"Nah," he refused quickly, "I want to do things right."

She looked at him with a puzzled inquisitive smirk. He hesitated to continue.

"I mean, nothing official or anything, but how would you feel about

maybe being my wife?"

Lilly covered her mouth to hide the huge smile that screamed "Yes!" without her saying a word.

"Just unofficially, hypothetically speaking?"

He probed for more of an answer knowing he didn't need one based on her initial reaction. He cut off any further response she could give with a solid questioning sort of demand. "Just think about it?" As he kissed her forehead, he rapidly rose.

Oliver grabbed the remaining box of beer, pulling out a few to leave behind.

"You really need to get a stove up in here, get some of those good

homecooked meals going on like you do so well.,"

he stated as he closed the back door behind him.

Lilly stood there for a moment taking in all that had just happened. He was definitely husband material: Strong, authoritative, and yet so considerate. She glowed inside, thinking of just how happy she would be to return the adoration he had shown. Without question, O had won her heart. As she headed to her room to complete arranging her closet, she touched the door frame of the hallway. This would be the same door frame that was photographed and placed in the divorce judge's manilla folder: blood stained, with a photo of her bruised swollen face and bleeding mouth just behind it. She walked down the hall enraptured in a delightful delusion of the perfect life with who she thought would be an amazingly loving husband. Her delusional oasis would soon become a barren desert.

CHAPTER XV

Terrorized Heart

"The LORD is my rock, my fortress, and my deliverer.
My God is my rock, in whom I take refuge, my shield,
and the horn of my salvation, my stronghold."

– Psalms 18:2- (BSB)

It had been 5 years of painful anguish. Lilly could never have imagined she would be in this place. She found herself overwhelmed with both terror and relief as she drove off, checking the rearview mirror to be sure he wasn't following her. Her heart pounded with fright; her head ached with confusion. What had come over him? So far gone into a disagreement that seemed to have lasted for days, the cause obliterated from her memory, she felt completely exhausted.

She refused the thought of being concerned about any of her belongings, especially her beautiful antique furniture, and the heirloom sewing machine that belonged to her great great grandmother. After all, he would probably destroy it along with everything else that was left.

After growing tired of the defenses, the silent attempts to eventually make him move on from his drunken rage, she recalled making a huge mistake

"I'm leaving you; I'm done.,"

she had said defeated as she sat looking at him in a state of rage. Oliver was raving mad and vocally defensive about how he couldn't stand one of the guys that refused to invite him to hangout because of the scene he had caused on their last outing.

He blamed her for everything, although he wouldn't confess to being a part of all that had gone wrong. When Lilly made the remark, he froze and went silent for a moment.

"What did you just say?" he questioned in disbelief.

"I just can't do this anymore with you," she surrendered.

"Oh, you think you're leaving?"

'O' quickly rushed to the kitchen and pulled a box cutter out of the utility drawer. He slid the blade out and she froze in hope of disappearing in her stillness and terror. Lilly knew that he was going to kill her. He began to destroy the furniture, slashing the sofa she was seated on first.

As tears of dread rolled down her cheeks, she was careful with every breath. She sat there stiff as if she had just seen a ghost. He cursed and guaranteed with actionable assurance that she would regret making, or even considering a separation. He would retaliate immediately, and Oliver made it clear that the consequences would not be at all favorable for her.

As he got lost in his terror strike, moving on to destroy his own antique lounge chairs and ottomans, Lilly got up enough courage to remove herself from the room. She knew that whatever she was going to do next, it would have to be quick. But what would she do? Hide, run? Both sounded like good options, but terror reminded her that she had to be strategic and fast.

Still watching him as he engaged in his malicious terror invoking exercise, she undetectably backed out of the kitchen and ran into the bedroom to grab a shoe box of important papers from under the bed. Lilly also grabbed a high heeled shoe to defend herself if need be as she made her break for the back door. She peaked into the living room, to find him facing the window out to the house across the street, still cursing, fussing, but now slashing the gold curtains. Carefully and quickly, she eased her way into the kitchen just enough to dart into the laundry room. Grabbing her purse that fortunately sat on the workbench by the back door, Lilly ran as fast as possible.

He would see her backing out of the driveway and chase her down in his rage! She instinctively knew it. Sure enough, just after backing out and putting the car in drive, there he was racing towards her from the backyard. With the pedal to the floor, the car peeled out! Lilly made a screeching turn at the first intersection to make sure he wouldn't catch her. She never ventured down any of the side streets in the neighborhood and was intentional about getting lost in unfamiliar territory. After a few lefts and rights, she needed to stop, find a place, and figure out what to do next. Lilly's heart raced and her body trembled so intensely, it was a struggle to gather her thoughts. She grabbed her phone and called one of her friends.

CHAPTER XVI

Reconciled to Bondage

"Let no one deceive you in any way, for it will not
come until the rebellion occurs and the man of
lawlessness- the son of destruction is revealed."

- 2 Thessalonians 2:3 – (BSB)

Months went by. She hated the idea of leaving
her home with everything she owned left behind.
Rumor had it that Oliver sold almost everything
that he hadn't destroyed. What he couldn't sell, he
gave away and supposedly moved in with an older
cousin. She missed him, the good part of him at
least: the gentleman that he used to be in the beginning when they had first met. It was too real, and
completely impossible for that side of him to just
not exist. There was unfortunately no trace of that
Oliver in the last few months she could recall. She
had high hopes that with time and space, he would
realize the error of his ways and seek help for his
problem. For months, Lilly refused to pick up her

phone to talk to him. She would only respond to text messages and the response would always be brief especially when it got ugly with name calling, or threats. That always seemed to be the case.

She refused to disclose her location. Allan contacted her wanting to resolve residential matters: unpaid rent, and handling of the security deposit. After he questioned her about her location, she discontinued the calls, and would respond only by text. Lilly knew that O was using his friend to get more information on her whereabouts. She had to be smart. Even his cousins and brother made attempts to contact her. She refused to engage in any means of conversation other than texting. Her messages were always sweet and simple, and she was careful not to disclose any pertinent information that would give away her whereabouts.

After some time and distance was put between them, the softer side of him would emerge. She was hesitant to hear him out at first, but eventually she softened as he disclosed his new commitment to doing better. He claimed to have stopped drinking and had begun counselling with a pastor that helped with substance abuse and domestic violence. He also claimed to have started attending the pastors church and invited her to come along one Sunday. After ignoring a few invitations, she finally agreed.

Lilly liked the church. It was a quaint old fashioned Baptist church, full of families that had history amongst the congregation. The mothers of the church were adorable: sweet, loving, and full of faith. After service they welcomed her with open arms as Oliver introduced her as his wife.

"She's beautiful, my goodness,"

raved Mother James, as she grabbed Lilly's hand to introduce her to the other Mothers in the church. Oliver smiled with pride and a sense of accomplishment as he stood watching Lilly meet their new church family. Mother James brought her back to where O had been conversing with a few of the deacons. She said,

"Get together you two, we're going to pray over you."

One of the deacons agreed as the congregation of men and women circled around them. After the head deacon led a strong prayer for reconciliation, and a strengthened bond, Lilly noticed Oliver weeping. In that moment, she saw a softer side of the gentleman that she had first met. She saw loneliness, regret, and loss in his eyes. His quivering lips struggled to straighten into a humble smirk. He seemed relieved that they were there together. His sincerity made her weep. O grabbed her into his arms with a strong embrace. They stood for quite a few minutes weeping together. The congregation around them could only give praise.

After agreeing on marital counselling, the pastor and his wife advised them to begin searching for a new home so that they could be fully reconciled within the next 3 months. Oliver wasted no time. They continued to live separately but would often meet for lunch or a walk in the park. Each time he saw her, he handed her a check with his monthly savings for the new home. Things seemed better. It appeared as though they were getting back on track in their relationship. O was always thoughtful and generous, gifting her dresses, jewelry, or shoes. He would take her on road trips to Florida, back to the town he had grown up in. They would shop at the malls or flea markets, meet up with some of his old friends for dinner, and then spend romantic passion filled evenings before heading back home.

They would never be able to find a deal quite like the house they had given up, but that wasn't as important as them getting back together as soon as possible. With what he had saved up, they settled for a small two-bedroom apartment in a rough area downtown. She and a few of her colleagues opened an office not far from there, so the location was perfect on nights Lilly had to work long hours. Oliver started taking classes online and relied on her heavily to complete assignments. She didn't mind. She loved being able to show care for him despite his flaws. Their pastor decided to start his own church, and it just so happened to be very close to their new home. They attended regularly and were very active in leading special programs: youth shut-ins, easter, and black history month. Many young members of the old congregation followed the pastor to the new location, so over time, they cultivated strong friendships with some of the couples and young adults. Everything was right on track, and they were right at home in the new church.

School has stressful for Oliver. He struggled to keep up with all the reading that was required for online courses and working overtime to try to eventually provide a better home for them. Lilly had taken on the responsibility of co-ownership of a business that required her to work lengthy hours. She took on some of his easy courses to assist him. At one point, he considered attending classes on campus in hopes that the in-person instruction would be more helpful than the self-learning that was required in the virtual environment. This would require cutting his hours at work, and he definitely didn't see that as an option with Lilly sometimes working 10–12-hour days. She didn't mind, but he did and quickly dismissed that option.

One Friday morning, Lilly prepared to go out of town to a business meeting. Her partners would meet her there and they planned to make it a short day. No one would want to go back to the office after traveling. She was excited about spending the early afternoon and evening with Oliver going into the weekend, so before departing, she prepared by completing all his class assignments. Lilly pulled some meat out of the freezer to thaw as she planned a nice home cooked meal: fried chicken, and fresh steamed broccoli, his favorite: homemade scalloped potatoes. It was sure to be a treat since they had both taken on so much responsibility with school, work, and church. Their quality time together suffered, so a relaxing weekend together would be perfect.

On her way to the meeting, Oliver called her and expressed his struggle with focusing on material for one of his entrepreneur classes. She smirked as she could sense his panic and desperation for her help.

"We'll take care of it when I get home. No sweat. Love you.,"

she assured him. She hoped that her reassurance would relax him even though her plans for the evening would be slightly skewed, but that didn't bother her. They would still have time together.

Lilly arrived for the meeting and met up with her partners Ellroy and Pat. They all went into the conference room and sat quietly taking notes during the presentation. Just before the first 15-minute break, Lilly felt herself getting feverish. Her nose was also a little runny. She went to the rest room and patted her face with a cool paper towel, sipped running water out of the palm of her hand, and headed back into the meeting. By the second hour, she had an uncontrollable sneeze. It reminded her of the time she sat in her Old Testament college class back in her youth and had a similar sneeze attack. Needless to say, both times, she had gotten so many 'God Bless You's' it was a total distraction to the presentation being given. Lilly got up to excuse herself and was followed out by Ellroy.

"Go on home Lil, we'll get some really good notes on the rest of the

meeting to fill you on Monday," he said.

Nodding in agreement, she headed towards her car. There would need to be a stop on the way in to get some medicine that could be taken once she reached home. Along the way, Lilly stopped behind a car that was checking the oncoming traffic for a break so it could turn left. The traffic coming in the opposite direction was steadily flowing, so she looked around at the area she didn't get to survey on her way to the meeting. Still waiting for the car in front of her to turn, Lilly happened to glance into her rearview mirror. Behind her was a rapidly approaching 16-wheeler. As it got closer to her, she realized that it was sure to hit her full force! There was no sign of it slowing down even at a few 100 feet behind her. She immediately became concerned about hitting the still vehicle in front of her yet to make its turn. Bracing herself for certain impact, Lilly prepared to turn off slightly to the right to avoid being sandwiched by the car ahead of her and the unrelenting truck. She squealed as she immediately heard the glass bust, and her knees hit the dashboard! In pain, she forced her leg down to stomp the brake pedal while trying to control the steering wheel. The huge truck dragged her screeching vehicle forward and slightly off the road. When her car finally came to a halt, she sat there petrified and trembling. Thank God she had just missed the car in front of her by a few feet. By the time she checked the rear mirror again, the driver of the truck was no longer visible through the big empty whole where the rear window once was. About 6 minutes passed before a police car arrived at the scene of the accident. Lilly was now calm enough to think clearly. She knew her knees would be bruised for sure. After bending to retrieve her purse from the passenger side floorboard, she pulled out her cell phone and dialed 911. Lilly attempted to give the dispatcher the details of the accident and her location using the highway name and a few landmarks. She was still a bit shaken up realizing that had her car hit the vehicle in front of her, she may not have survived. Just as she began to gain a sense of gratitude, Lilly felt a sense of déjà vu. Suddenly, her conscious mind recalled an old dream of her driving down a highway. She remembered that as she drove, her car's engine suddenly stalled out and just as suddenly reignite. In the dream, it kept happening, and she thought to herself "This is dangerous, a really big truck can kill me." She recalled turning off to the right of the highway as a huge truck zoomed past her. The recollection amazed Lilly with a gasping awe. She got lost in time for a lengthy moment, thinking about what she could have suffered had she not been so blessed to have survived this. Back in the old dream, she saw a huge gray house on the opposite side of the road bank far across a shimmering lake. There was a park bench alongside a brownish red trodden path dusted with autumn leaves. The path inclined uphill in a fall hinted forest. Suddenly, she jumped out of the trance and looked up to see Ellroy tapping on the window of her car.

"Lily, Lily! Are you okay?" he exclaimed with a terrorized look.

Before long she was gazing at a gorgeous clear blue sky that looked as if God had backstroked his white paint-dipped hands across it. The sun wasn't in her direct sight, but its peripheral presence made her squint, and the warmth of it made her feel protected. The wind blew her hair across her face as she laid flat on the stretcher. It was as if the soft fingertip of an angel brushed her cheek. Her spirit was quieted by that loving familiar presence of Him. She remembered Him.

CHAPTER XVII

Accidental Backslide

"In all your ways acknowledge Him, and
He will make your paths straight."

- Proverbs 3:6 -(BSB)

As Lilly came out of the medically induced trance that she had been in for some time, she sat up to see Elroy's arms folded as he conversed with a nurse. He turned and looked at his friend with a smile,

"Okay Lil let's get you home. You're gonna be just fine. You'll

probably be sore, but they got you some pain meds and a follow up

appoint for Monday."

She immediately thought about Oliver. Elroy followed behind Lilly as the nurse wheeled her out of the room, through a few back halls and out to a lobby area. As Elroy went to retrieve the car, she noticed it was evening already and thought to call O, but being a bit lethargic from the medication, the call could wait. Elroy pulled up and the nurse wheeled her to the curbside to carefully helped her up and into the car. Lilly thanked Elroy for taking the time to wait with her just before she slipped back into a deep sleep.

A few hours later, Elroy nudged her awake as he pulled up to her apartment. She saw O standing in the window, thanked Elroy again, and exited to get inside. Oliver met her at the door.

"I've been worried sick. Did you think to check your phone?"

He stepped back to let her in and just as he shut the door, the foul language and rage spewed out of him. Lilly immediately began to cry recalling how she was so close to not surviving the wreck. She began to explain the horror of how she had been in a near death collision. Just as she went to have a seat, Lilly saw the large bottle of cheap vodka sitting on the floor next to the chair by the window. O apparently had been waiting for her while relapsing into a drunken state.

She sensed trouble right away! Lilly hadn't thought to call him until it was too late, and she would regret that mistake. He began to verbally assault her, showing no empathy for her horrific ordeal. O was loud, insensitive, and demeaning, blaming her for wrecking the car and for not being home in time to help him finish his assignment.

She couldn't believe he had relapsed. Triggered by the circumstances, she became afraid to speak or defend herself. As she wept, she closed her eyes, laid back and silently began to pray. After a few minutes of attempting to provoke her to respond, he gave up. Oliver disappeared into the bathroom to relieve himself, then reappeared and observed her doing what he would consider sleeping. He grabbed his bottle and took a seat in silence.

He stared out of the window and within a half hour fell into a deep sleep. Lilly was careful not to wake him. She eased into their bedroom and got undressed then stared out of the window as she watched the lights of the cars driving by. The dreaded sight of the liquor store 4 blocks away vexed her soul. It glamourized the poison liquid that had stolen her redeemed happiness once again.

Lilly wanted to act as if this had never happened, and maybe it would be forever forgotten. She stood for a while staring out the window at the parked cars hopeful that his behavior wouldn't get any worse. Forgiveness had to be extended and charging the relapse to the stress he had been enduring was the best way to mentally cope. She had faith that this behavior wouldn't escalate.

Lilly stood there peering out of the window that would months later be shattered on the very ground she stood on, giving clear view to the flashing police lights right where the parked cars were. She would be standing there just a few months from now with no hope and agonizing sorrow. Her faith would be crushed as she would soon watch the police cuff her husband and press his head down and into the back of a patrol car. Her eyes and face would be throbbing from the impact of his heavy fists.

CHAPTER XVIII

Death's Defeat

"You, little children are from God and have
overcome them, because greater is He who
is in you than he who is in the world."

-1 John 4:4 -(BSB)

The initial relapse was followed by months of re-
gression, escalated incidents, loss of employment,
and demotion from the deacon board. Lilly also
suffered from the embarrassment and humiliation
of being considered the loud neighborhood brawl-
ers who couldn't keep it civil.

Oliver drifted away from church attendance after
the pastor refused to bail him out of jail for a second
time. He was extremely resentful toward Lilly, who
gained the sympathy of the entire congregation
after two physical assaults. In between assaults, Oliver was privately reprimanded by the pastor after
showing up to a church block party with heavy al-

cohol on his breath.

One of the brothers at church worked for a dealership. The pastor was gracious enough to provide the down payment and first few car notes on a new car to replace the one that was wrecked. Within 3 months, Oliver totaled the car driving drunk.

The domestic violence had gotten so bad, the landlord refused to extend their lease. It would expire in 4 months, so they had to find a new place to live. Oliver was nonchalant about the whole situation, not taking ownership for any of the turmoil he had caused. It was quite the paradox. He took a hard stance in blaming everyone else for every mishap that he had caused. Lilly began to realize that his issues stemmed deeper than alcoholism, maybe bipolar disorder, or narcissism.

It was very discouraging to watch his health decline so rapidly. Oliver had jaundice eyes on rare occasions when he was sober. They would always be blood shot in the morning or when he got drunk. Drunkenness had turned into a daily occurrence. O slowly began to lose control of his bowel movements. The thief of intoxication was a strong ally for death. Lilly felt broken and defeated. She wanted him to get help, but she lost all hope when the pastor said candidly,

"Sweetheart, if God can't help him, there's no help for him."

She prayed for him to give up the drinking, but every month it seemed to get worse. She managed to move them into a nice quaint little cottage that sat right in front on a small lake. It was a quiet cutter neighborhood, out of immediate proximity of any liquor store, but he'd always find a way to get the poison.

It got so bad that one night, a neighbor found him passed out on the sidewalk in front of a bus stop, gathered him up, and brought him home. Oliver fell into the house just as Lilly opened the door. She dragged him to the nearby sofa, covered him with a blanket, and went to her room to pray.

Just like the pastor said, God would indeed be the only one that could help, and she had to make sure that God heard her plea. As much as O had hurt her, she knew it was deeper than that. She resented Oliver for all the pain and embarrassment he had caused her, yet she refused to stand by and just watch him slowly kill himself. Lilly prayed, because it was all that was left. During this tough time, she had lost her grandmother who knew nothing of the tumultuous ordeal. Then, a few weeks later, her pastor passed away. Without his mentorship, she felt completely hopeless, even in continuous prayer. At that point, her primary prayer request was to be able to escape the nightmare with her own life.

CHAPTER XIX

Called From the Grave

"More than that, I count all things as
loss compared to the surpassing excellence
of knowing Christ Jesus my Lord, for who I
have lost all things. I consider the rubbish that
I my gain Christ and be found in Him."

- Philippians 3:8-9- (BSB)

Years had gone by. Lilly found herself in a huge
breath-taking park, not far from the sanctuary
where she would often go to pray. She sat on the
vibrant green grass and peered out across the rippling glossy lake. There was a magnificent view of a
grand slate gray 3 or 4 story home which sat on the
opposite bank. It appeared stately with its imperial
white windowpanes. The foundation sat hidden
beyond the wild thick foliage of bushes that created
a ridged forest border peaking low from the left and
towering to the right. The grounds of the home re-

mained mysterious. It was easy to imagine the elegance of the landscape, and the sophisticated modern architecture. In a clearing of the thick foliage to the right was a neighboring white home, slightly taller, with large protruding bay windows on the upper floor. A chandler hung inside a screened in porch on the lower floor. Tall round elegant lamp posts stood in perfect symmetry to the center of the property, and the wild thick foliage hid all else in sight.

To the left was a beige home, just as grand in size. The dark roof top shingles shielded it from the open sun. It wasn't as stately as the other two homes, but its proximity to the other estates could only mean the hidden landscape in the front of the property was a sight to behold. Unlike the other homes, it sat on an angle making it apparent that the property was on a cul de sac, which gave it the appearance of an island. Its forest covered borders with clearings that led to the back of the estates met a few neighboring docks on the lake.

Lilly got up to travel the meandering hiking trails as part of her daily routine. As she crossed the paved narrow roadway to get to the trail's entrance, she headed down a brownish red trodden path dusted with autumn leaves. Off to the side of the pathway was a park bench. As Déjà vu struck her, she stopped in her tracks and looked back at the lake. Her Canaan? It was so similar to a dream scene she used to gaze upon, but much grander. As many times as Lilly had been to this same location, she had never noticed any familiarity. A divine hunch made her look up at the sky she hadn't thought to examine before and to her amazement, it appeared as if God had backstroked it with His white paint-dipped fingers forming lines of clouds. She lifted her sunglasses on to her head. As the scene brightened, the warmth of the sun gave her a sense of familiar protection. Lilly breathed deep and took in a fresher perspective as her body absorbed the warmth and brightness of the sunlight. In that moment she recognized His powerful presence.

The wind blew her hair against her face as if her locks had been lifted by the fingertip of an angel gently stroking her cheek. She felt a sense of gratitude. He had gone before her, behind her, and was presently reminding her that He would forever be by her side. She allowed her spirit to be lovingly and freely twirled around in His dance.

She began more and more to enjoy what to the world looked like singleness. God amazingly revealed His presence to her just as he did when she was younger; after lifting her out of bondage, delivering her from the demonic forces that were sure to come for her life right after they had taken Oliver. God walked and talked with her daily as she found Him each waking day in His Word, in His promises, and in the world around her. In her quiet intimate moments with Him, He showed her their future: His purpose for her life, and glimpses of His plans for her life. He became the unfailing authority that she looked for in Oliver, but so much more. He stripped her desire for everything except what pleased Him, and she could genuinely appreciate it. Everything paled in comparison to Him. There was nothing He required her to forsake; no extreme she would go through to replicate His love, forgiveness, and grace. He became more than present. He was alive, by way of His promises, His faithfulness, His calling her by name. He openly wed her and changed her name, pouring out living waters of blessing on her. Lilly was now able to carry herself in a humble confidence, and it was evident that she was regal in Him. She lived surrendered and fully submitted to Him.

That evening she rode up the long swerving road which was set in the midst of sloping hills. The sky had a peachy purple hue as the sun began to set. The winding road home was fenced on both sides by enormous dogwood trees speckled with vivid white flowers. The treetops arched and met almost perfectly in the center of the street. As she drove through, the white pedals that had fallen from the trees danced on the ground along with the wind. She pulled up to the top cul de sac at the very end of the road to reach home. As she stepped out of the car, Lilly was immediately struck with the sensual scent of the dogwood trees. She looked back down the road from which she had just travelled and it reminded her of a long flower sprinkled wedding isle, beautiful with its natural white arch. In that moment she realized that He was there waiting for her. He would always be there. He had always been there.

Outside of the seven long painful years of bondage; outside of suppressing many years of denial; outside of forcing justification for the sake of reverencing a few, but dear and happy memories; outside of the intense withdrawals of loneliness, Lilly was far gone from overwhelming depression that made her question how she could continue to face the world; far gone from hoping inside of an impossible love. This is where she stood. She stood enraptured by the very presence of God. Once more, lovesick and in awe, she stood overwhelmed by an immense gratitude for each and every exhaled breath. Moreover, she was continually extended the ability to repeat that same grace. She drew in the spirit that was breathing on her. He welcomed her, and Lilly received Him with thanksgiving. Each day, He infiltrated her heart and penetrated her spirit until she fluttered with weakness. One could say she acquiesced to an intrusive submission that made all she ever was and all that she ever would be, yield to His power: A power more than worthy of serving; a power that was Almighty and irrevocable; a power majestically strong; a power that encapsulated all of these characteristics, yet concurrently remained gentle. She would always know Him. Lilly was experiencing a brush of His euphoria in her innermost yearning all over again, but never again would it be forgotten; audacious in its necessity; brazen that her natural stance was founded on it, inside of the insight of eternity. It was her unveiling.

She was inside of falling outside of herself and falling out of love with all but His power. This omnipotent and glorious presence managed to erase all memory of pain and humiliation, every anger and unworthy feeling, every distrust, and all the things that made her die to abundant life. A feathering sensation that started from an inhaled breath, not exhaled at once. A breath withheld and overcome by His penetrating Spirit that gently stroked her at the sides of her breast. It traced the shape of her hips until her feet were weak and unsteady, until they trembled with uncertainty, until she felt as if they could no longer hold her upright. Yet the Spirit which paralyzed her flesh was indeed able to thrust her into the heights of heaven. An old, yet familiar Spirit that came with a newness afresh to weaken her. To pounce upon and revive her soul straightaway. As she bowed her head and shoulders in submission to be overcome, she recognized that she had fully died to all that she was. The saturating Spirit blew with force, until she cried out to rebirth all that would become. Right there, as she surrendered her life again, Lilly also surrendered all of her past. She surrendered all of her present and all of her future. Her heart had been raised from the dead. She would love like never before and like never again and forever more. Inside of His mighty arms, her spirit was re-born to newness of life. Her soul would live again as though it were buried alive. All of this He would continue to reveal; to pour into; to speak to her "Resurrected Heart."

"When all has been heard, the conclusion of the matter is this: Fear God and keep His commandments, because this is the whole duty of man. For God will bring every deed into judgment, along with every hidden thing, whether good or evil."

- Ecclesiastes 12:13-14- (BSB)

AFTERWORD

As I sat in a relationship skills class listening to the executive director of a non-profit organization, she began to focus on domestic violence prevention. Suddenly, the statement she made snatched me back to the foundation of it all:

"Absence of injury has nothing to do with safety."

There I was as if it were only yesterday; staring at the Facebook Friend-Anniversary of myself and a woman I once worked with. She had just been murdered by her husband a few days prior. It shocked me to my core as the director's statement jarred me back in thought! I had known her husband personally, as they both worked for me in an Insurance Office a few years back. He was always kind and gentle in nature, in fact, he would bring me a dozen Joseph's Coat roses every year on my birthday. As I continued drifting into deeper memories, I recalled teasing the wife often. Whenever I gestured that she shouldn't allow her hubby to be such a charming flirt, she would respond with a non-cha-

lant chuckle claiming his harmlessness. In knowing and working with them both, I was inclined to
agree. The old man was a gentle soul, so it appeared.
Judging this book by its cover proved to be a deadly
mistake!

I remembered standing there, holding my phone,
and looking at her lovable face as I searched my
memory for signs that I may have missed: a bruise,
a distraught demeanor, a verbal clue, or overlooked
context in conversation. There was nothing I could
recollect at all. She was gone, and I was immersed
in such an intentional disbelief, not wanting this
tragedy to be anyone's reality: not the husband who
would have to live with what he had done, and not
the children that would have to live without their
mother and grandmother. I longed to dismiss the
aftermath of the tragedy; the guilt over things I had
never detected as signals or flags in their normal
looking marriage. As I mustered up the grit to dive
back into my own painful past, I knew I needed help
to regurgitate it all; to bring to fruition a glimpse
of my own difficult yet triumphant testimony, God
would have to speak to my heart!

One beautiful Sunday morning as I walked out
of a church sermon entitled 'Hearing from God', I
ventured right into the midst of his voice. After
service, I walked into a quaint little French brunch
spot for a pre birthday celebration with one of my
dear friends. As I looked to find where she was

seated, my attention was diverted to discover a single Joseph's Coat rose on nearly every table in that restaurant. I immediately acknowledged God's still quiet voice. I heard Him gently speak to my heart, my soul, and every fiber of my being: this work must be completed. I heard the husband's soul cry out for repentance; I heard the wife's soul silently screaming for help all along. That was the confirmation I so desperately needed. My story was relevant, critical, and necessary, but God needed me to know it wasn't just my story.

I completed this work on Resurrection Sunday of 2021. Exhausted with the attempts to relive the horrors of my own abusive marriage, I realized that I needed to recuperate with a girl's trip. As my son in law drove me and another dear friend to the airport to board a flight out of the country, he was overjoyed that I had finally completed the book you have just read. I testified how the woman's death, the sight of the roses, and God's voice all bound the pages of this work so tightly together. We spoke of my intentions while away: to relax, pray, and hear from God about what was next for my life.

One evening towards the end of the vacation, I met a curious young gentleman in the resort lounge. Through our conversation, I enthusiastically shared my testimony of how God delivered me from an abusive seven-year marriage. As my friends and I got up to call it a night, the phone rang. We stood bewildered at the news, literally frozen in shock! One of the women that should have accompanied us on the trip had been murdered by her husband: shot 13 times in front of their two young daughters! It was God's voice again, this time with an authority that I had not heard before. Although He wasn't shouting, His firm voice resonated over the agonizing screams of his daughter's desperate soul. There was no next instruction for me at that point, and there would never be a next abusive episode in my journey ahead. This would forever be a holy discontent for me; forever be a cause I would advocate for. I made it through my abuse for a reason, and because I survived, others will live as well; others will dream again; others will find love, joy, and peace through the Blood of Jesus. This is the story of the survivor, the redeemed, the resurrected daughter and bride of Christ. This is our story. Let us be washed. Let us rejoice in our "Resurrected Hearts"!

Isaiah 54:5-7 (NIV)

For your Maker is your husband- the Lord Almighty is his name-the Holy One of Israel is your Redeemer; he is called the God of all the earth. The Lord will call you back as if you were a wife deserted and distressed in spirit- a wife who married young, only to be rejected, says your

God, "For a brief moment I abandoned you, but with deep compassion I will bring you back."

If you need help contact the National Domestic Violence Hotline at 1-800-799-SAFE (7233)

Or Text "Start" to 88788

Email inquiries or comments to wordwashedheart@gmail.com

REFERENCES

The Holy Bible: Berean Study Bible [BSB]. 2016. 1st edition. http://

biblehub.com/bsb/genesis/1.htm

The Holy Bible: New Living Translation [NLT]. 2013. Carol Stream:

Tyndale House Foundation. Tyndale House Publishers, Inc.

https://www.biblegateway.com/versions/New-Living-trans-

lation-NLT-Bible/#booklist.

The Holy Bible: New International Version [NIV].

1984. Grand Rap-

ids: Zonderman Publishing House. https://www.biblegateway.

com/versions/New-International-Ver-sion-NIV-Bible/#book-

list.

Made in the USA
Columbia, SC
12 February 2022

55299631R00087